HAIR
COLORING BOOK

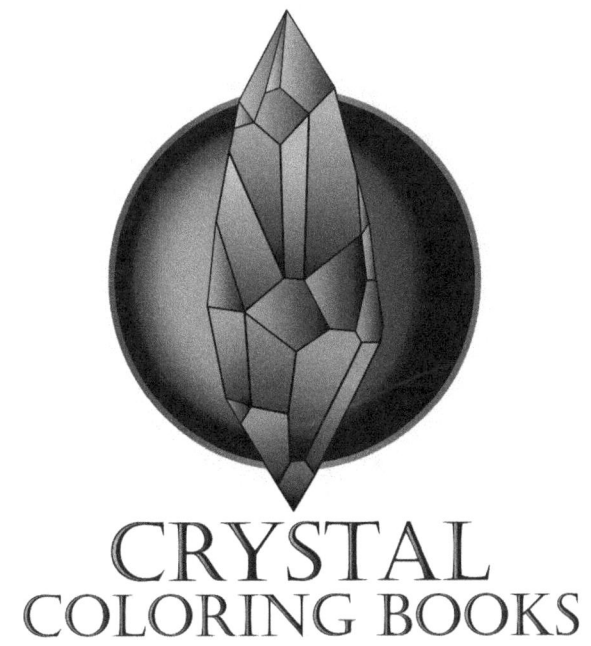

CRYSTAL
COLORING BOOKS

ISBN-13: 978-1546953241
ISBN-10: 1546953248

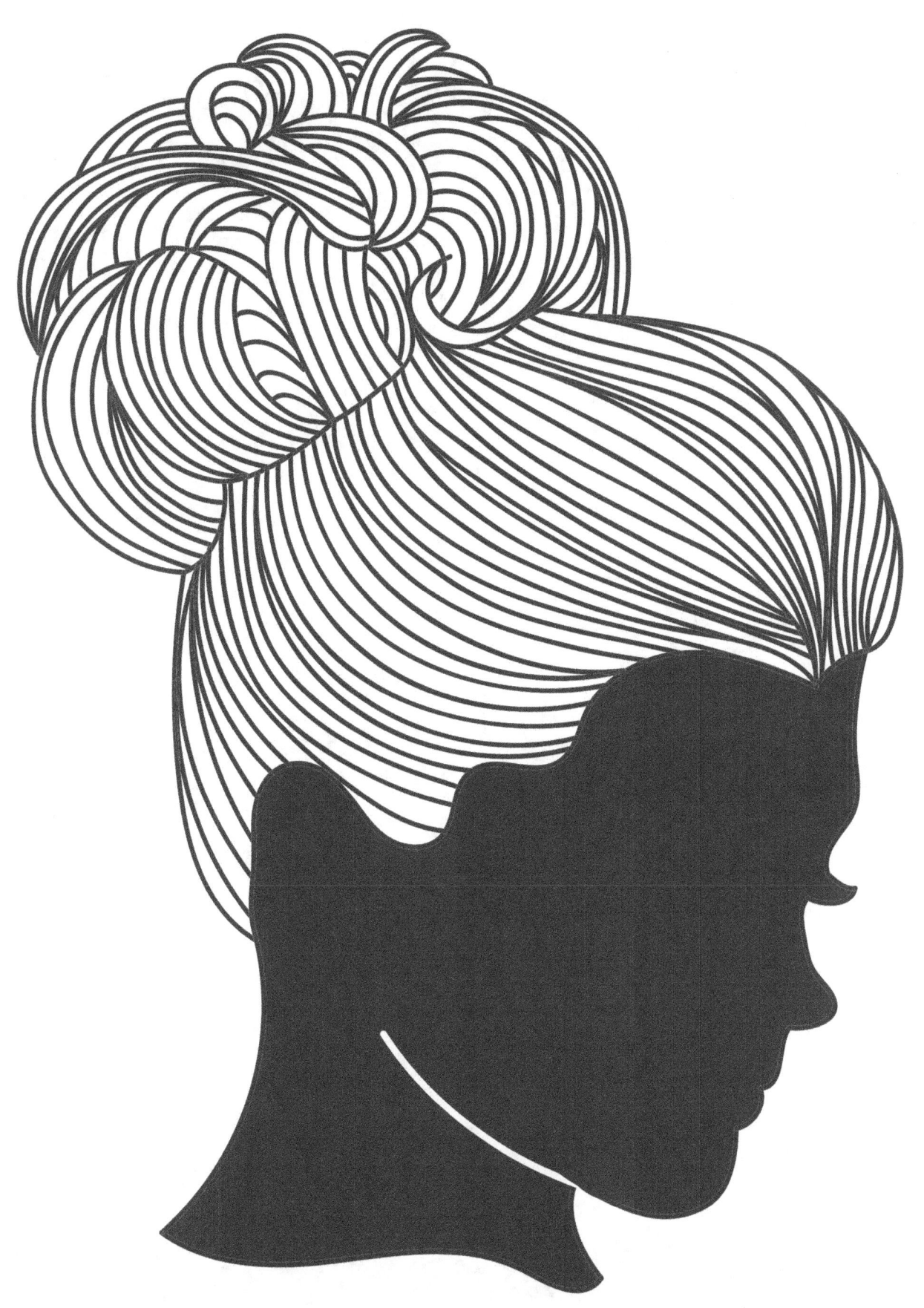

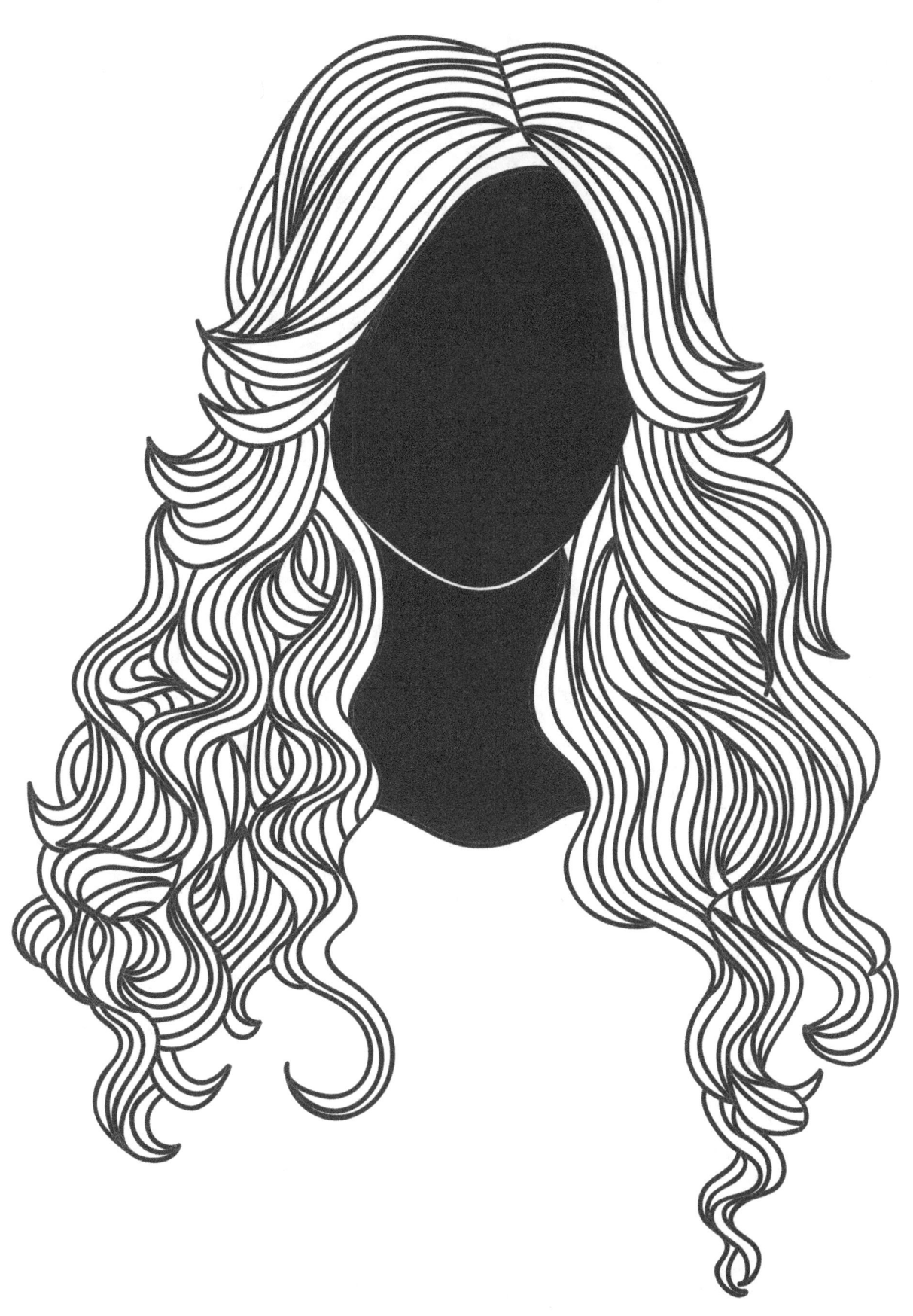

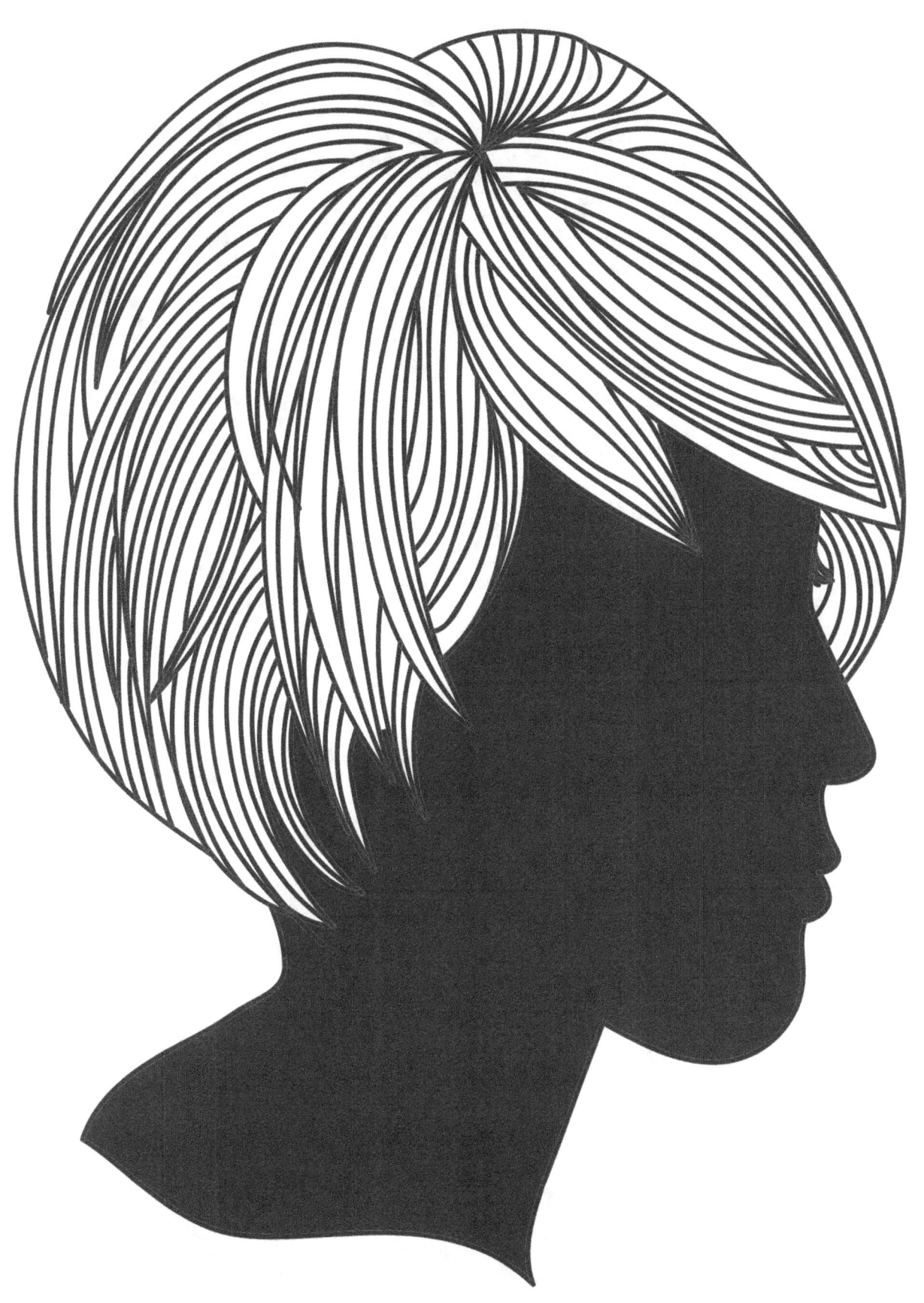

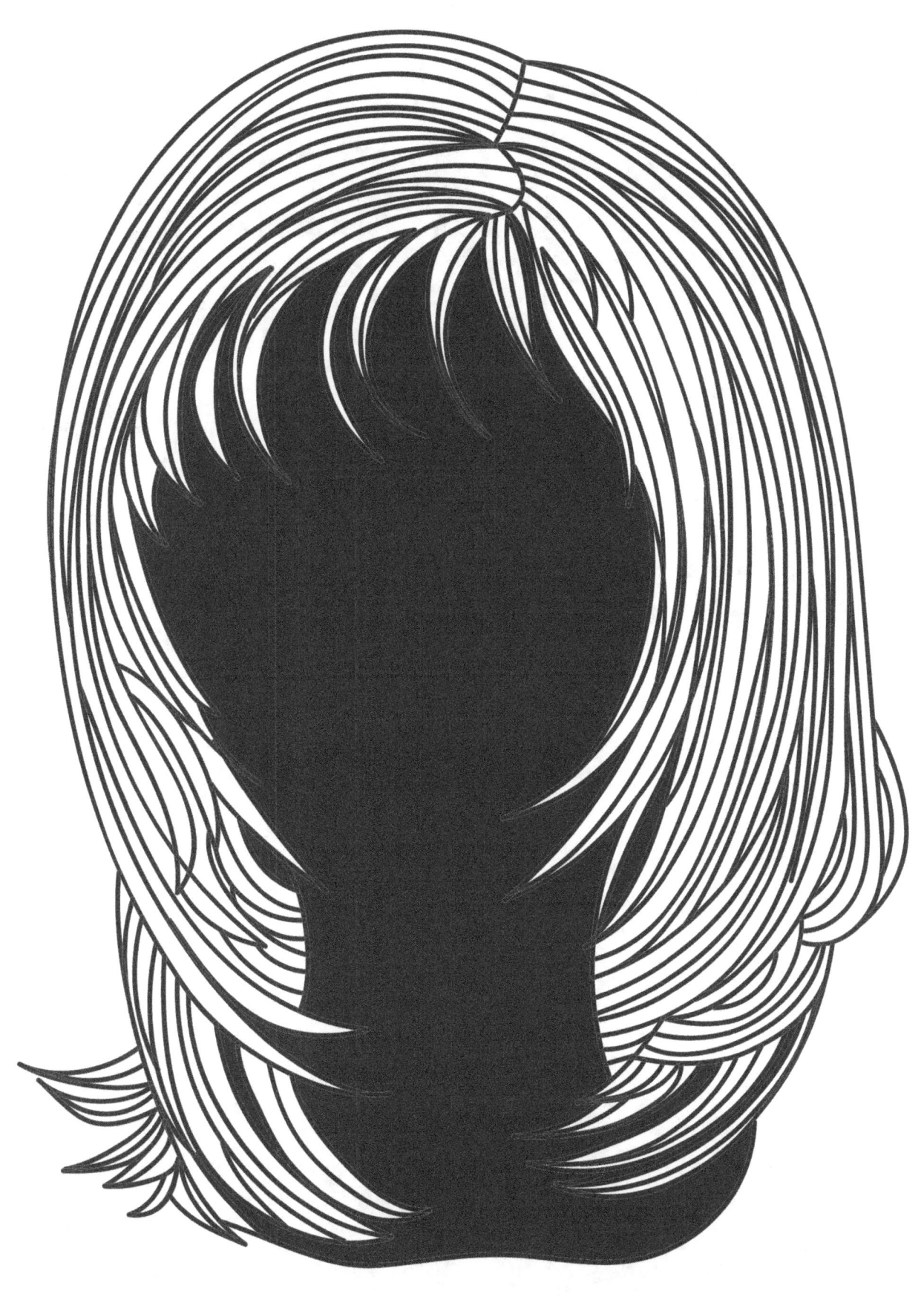

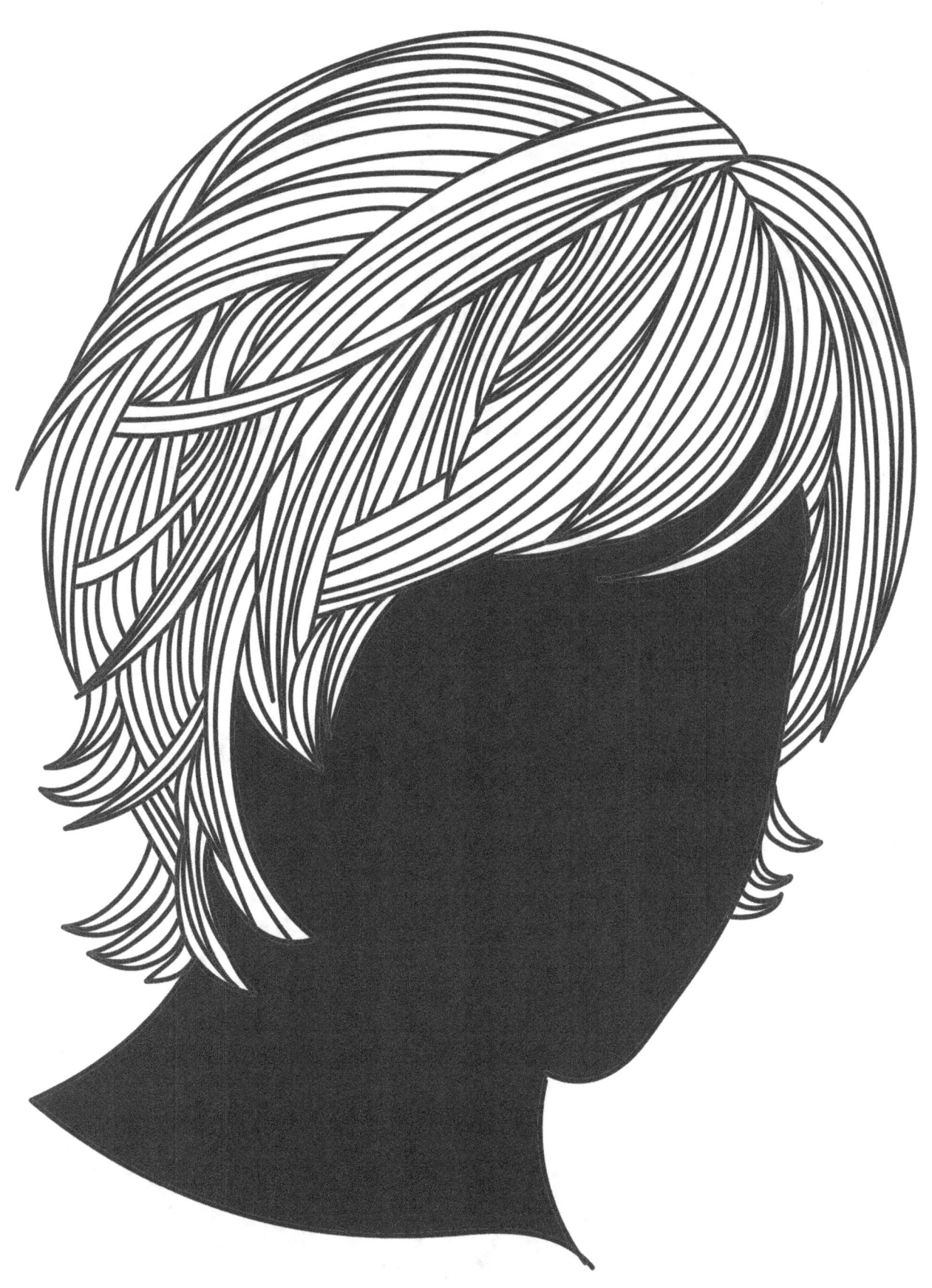

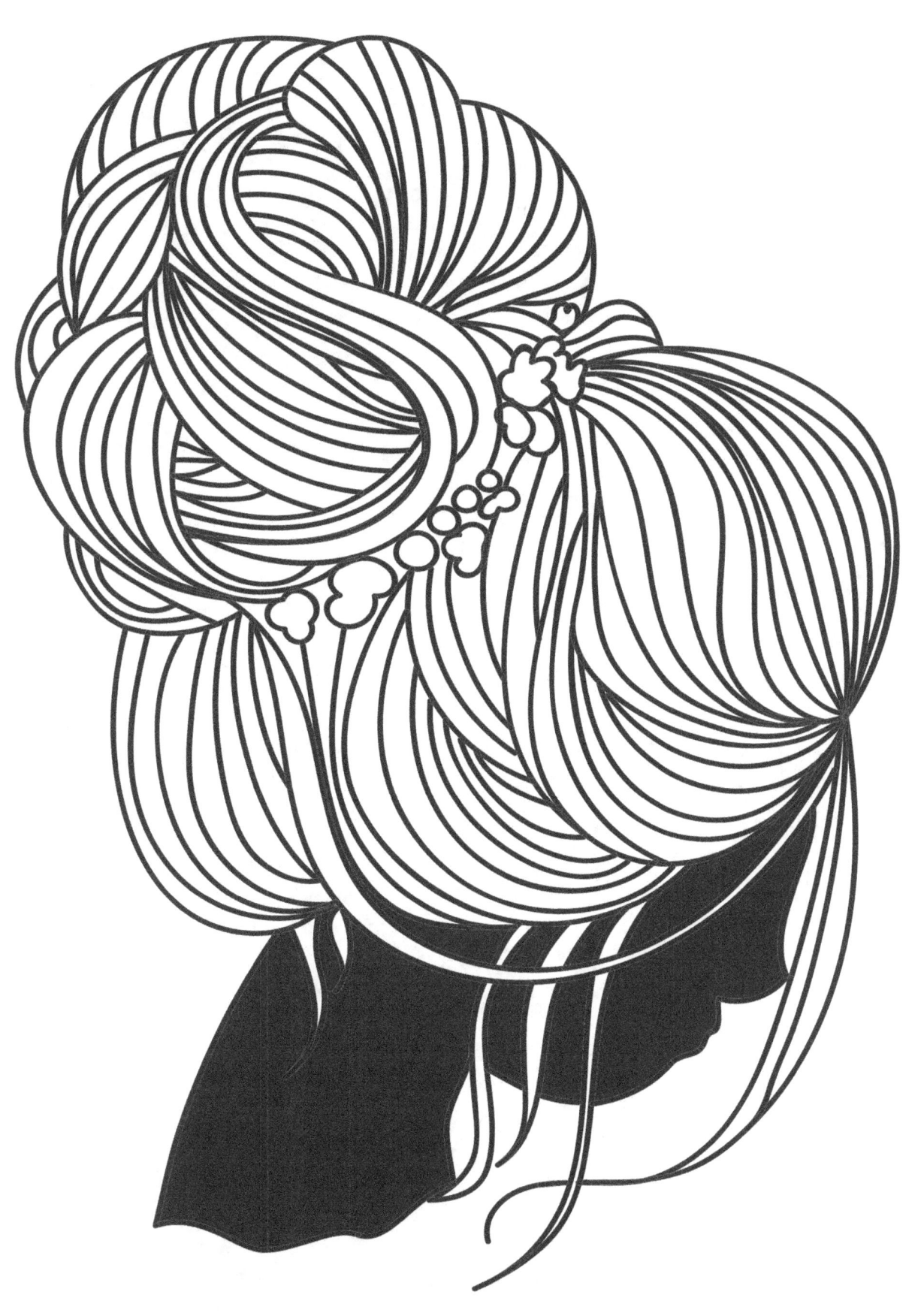

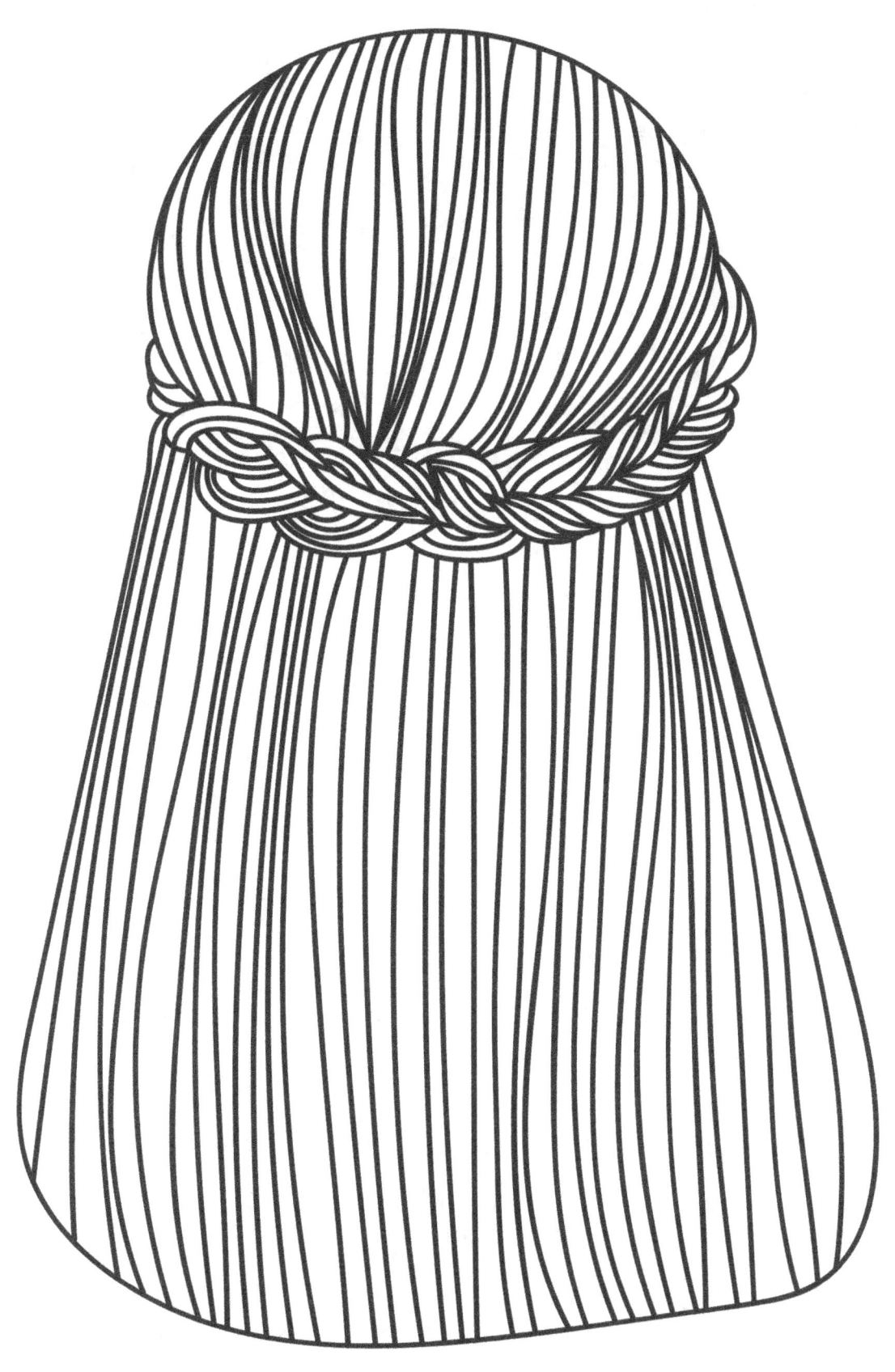

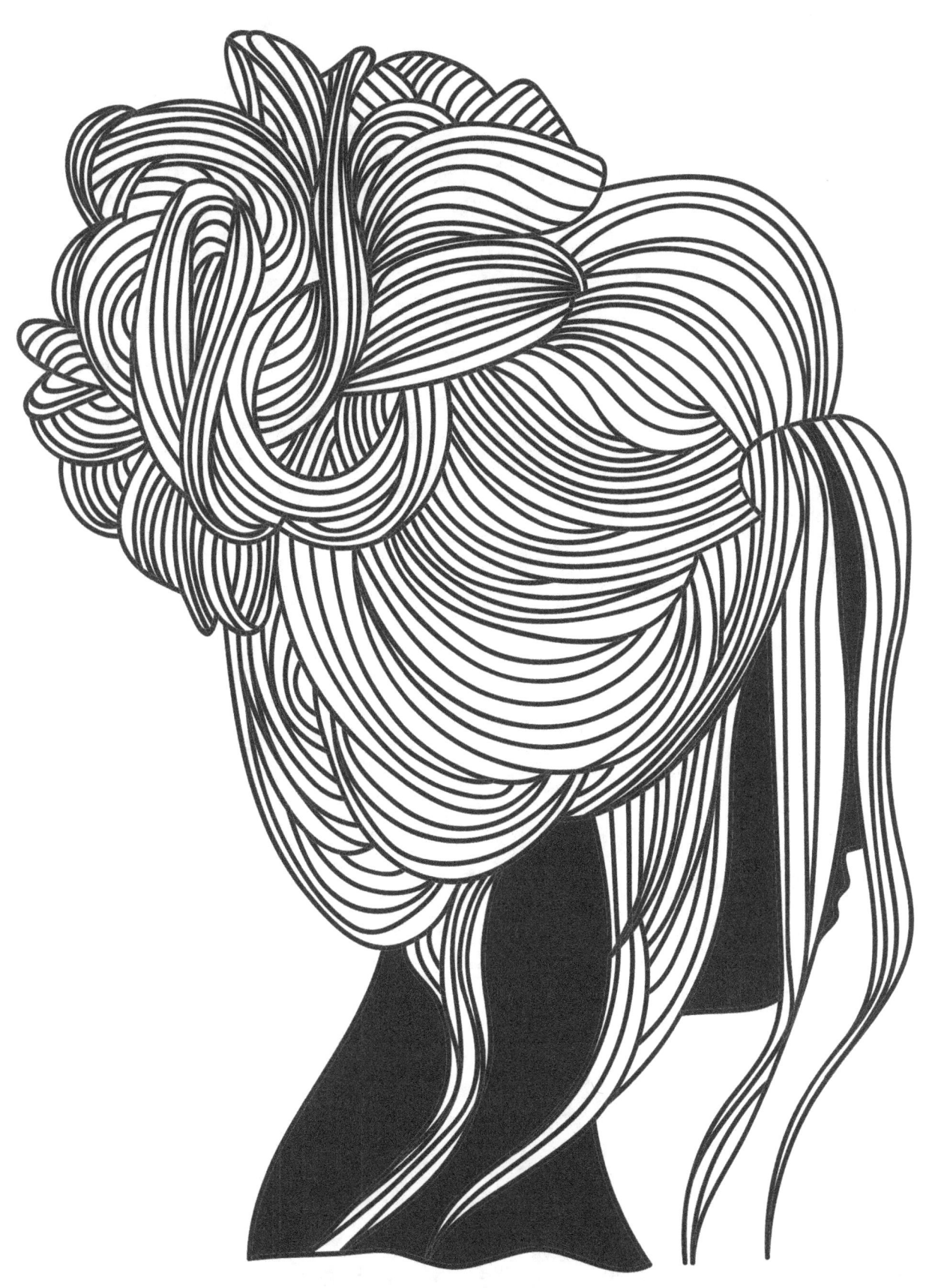

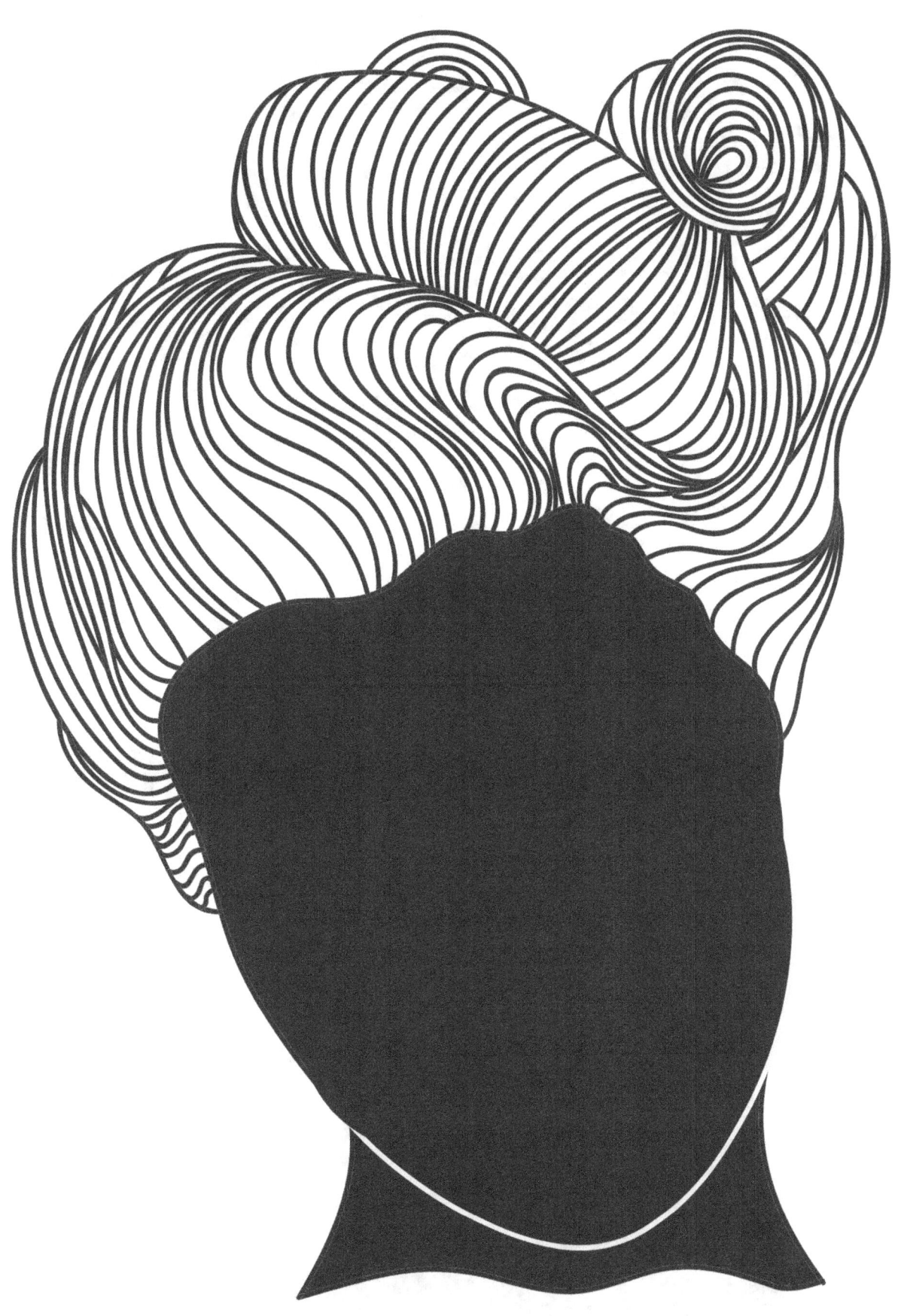

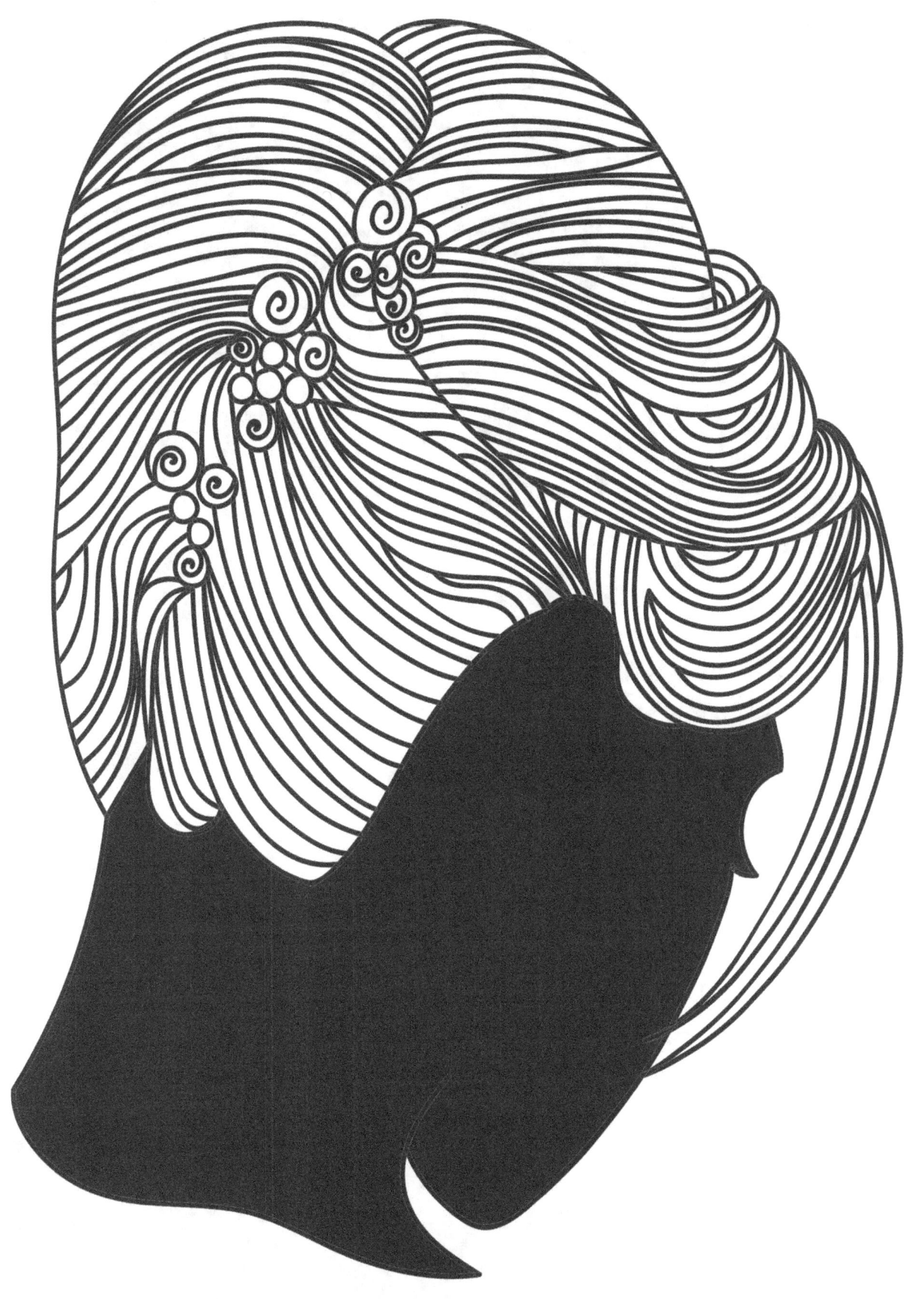

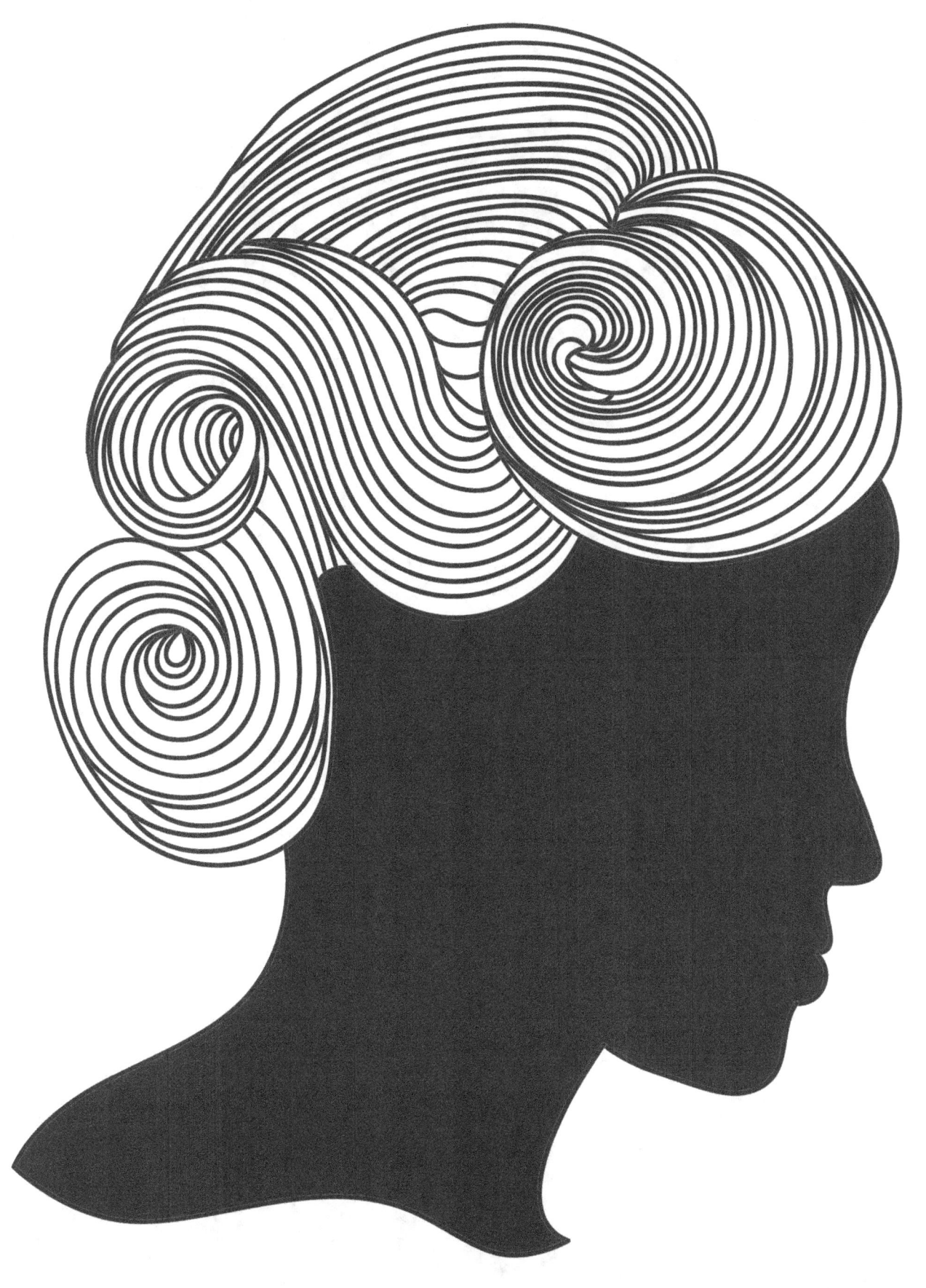

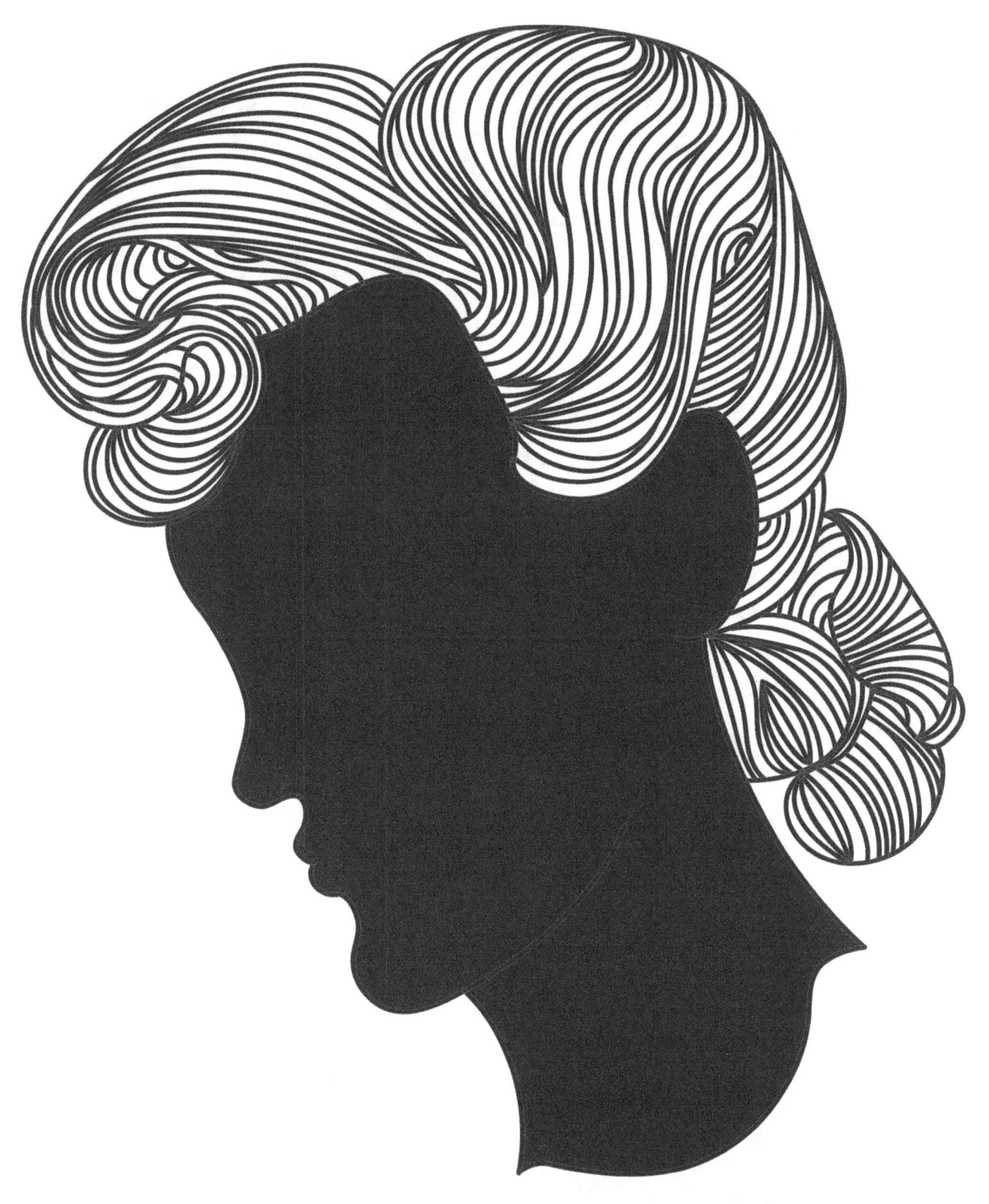

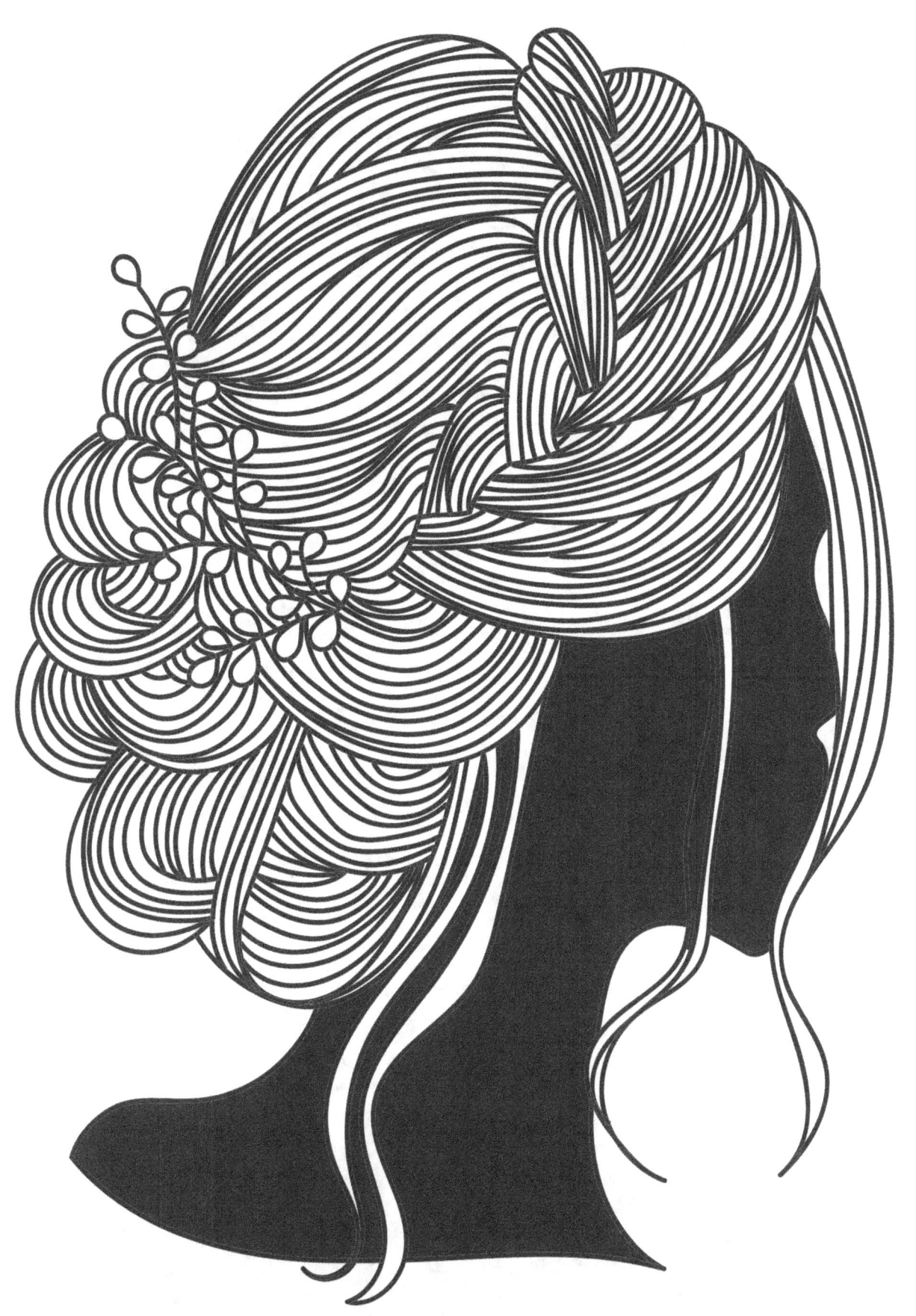

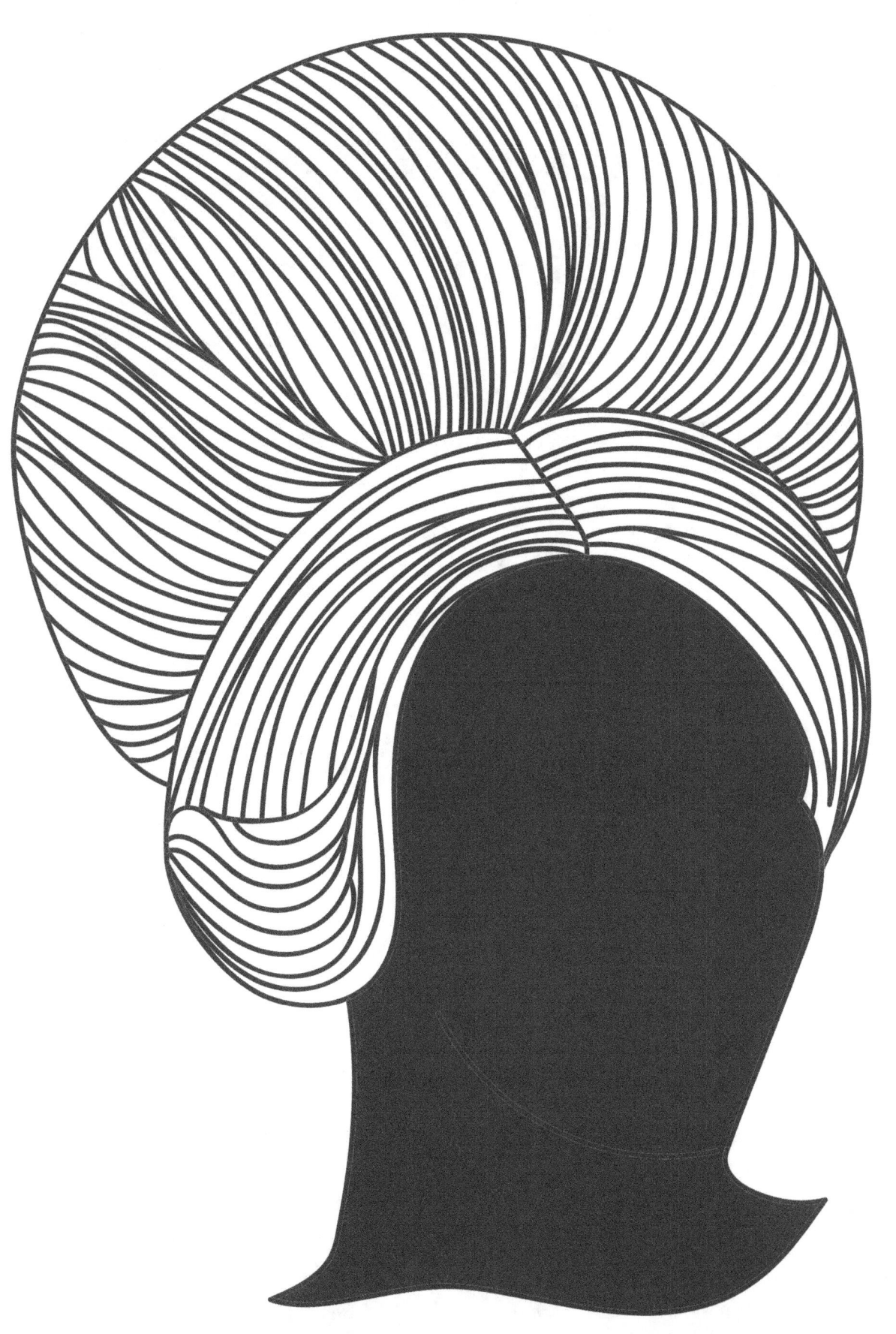

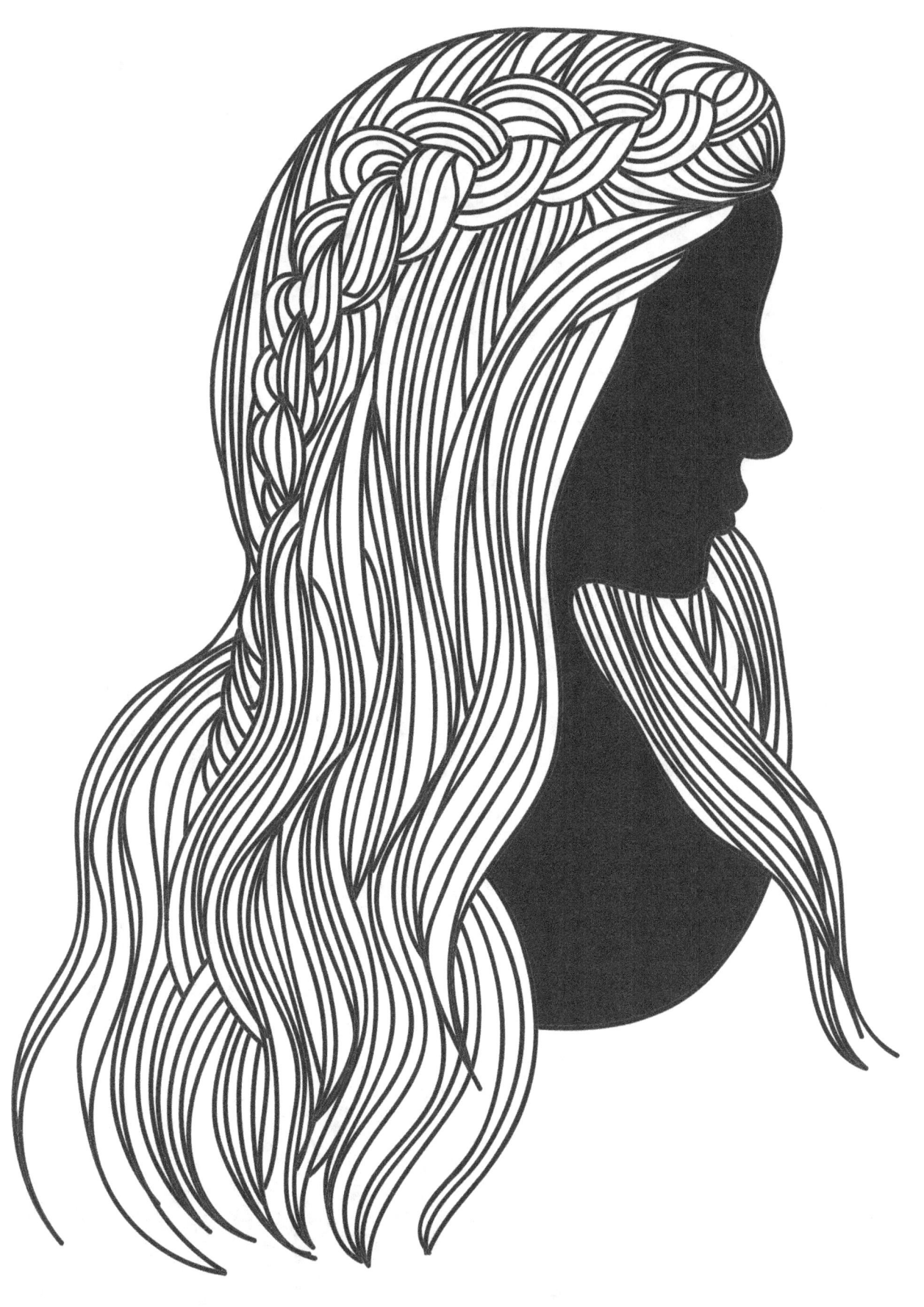

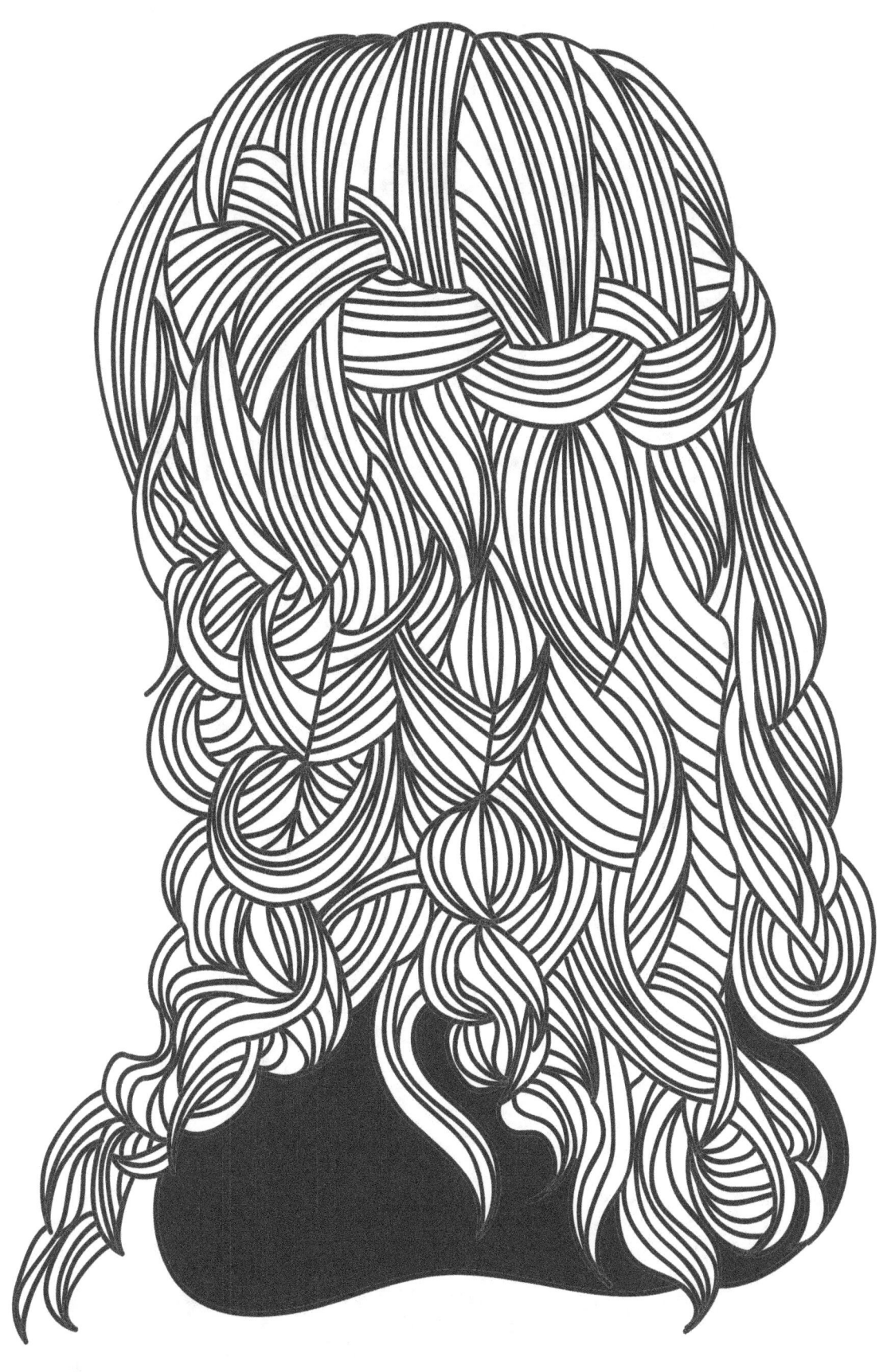

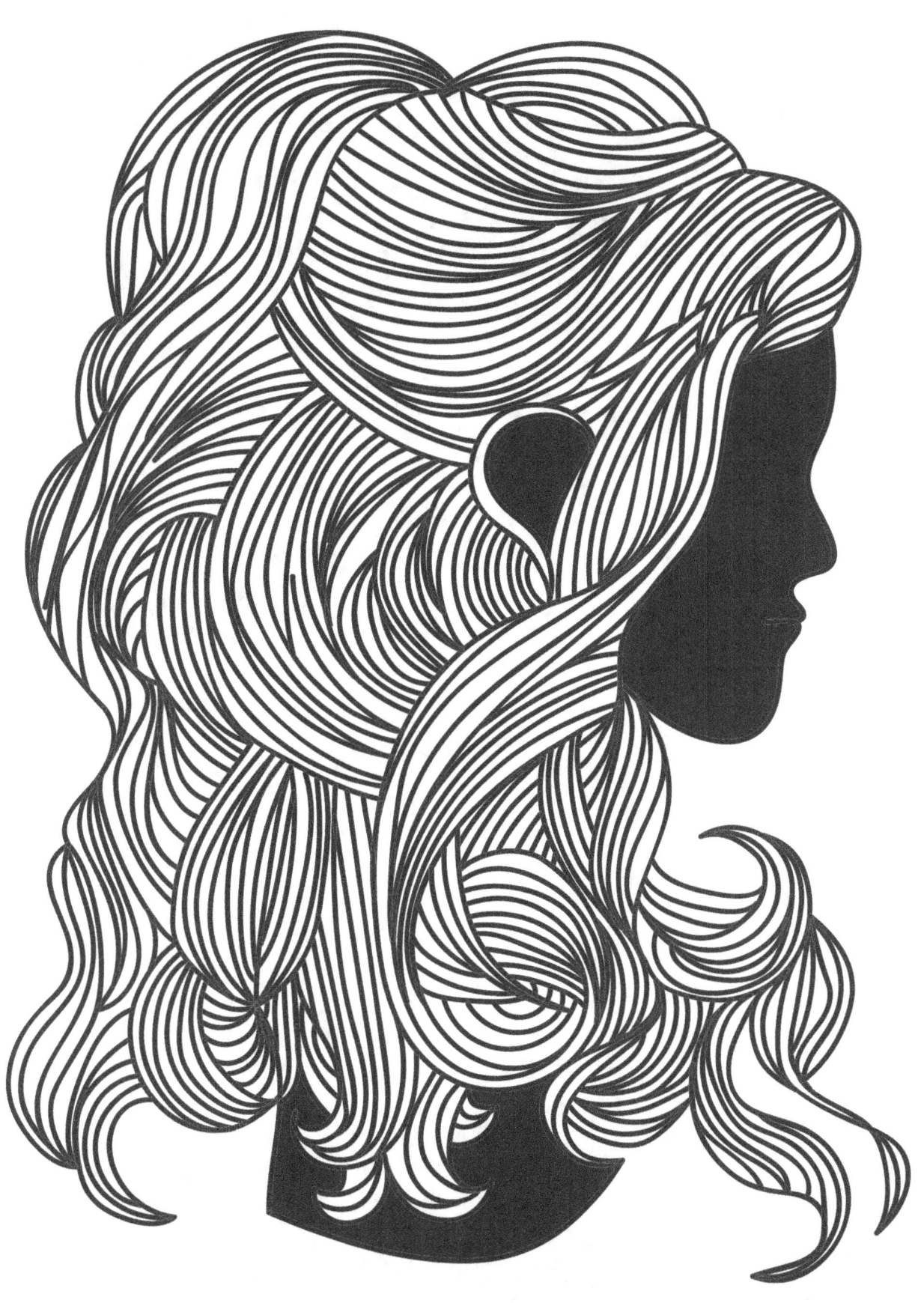

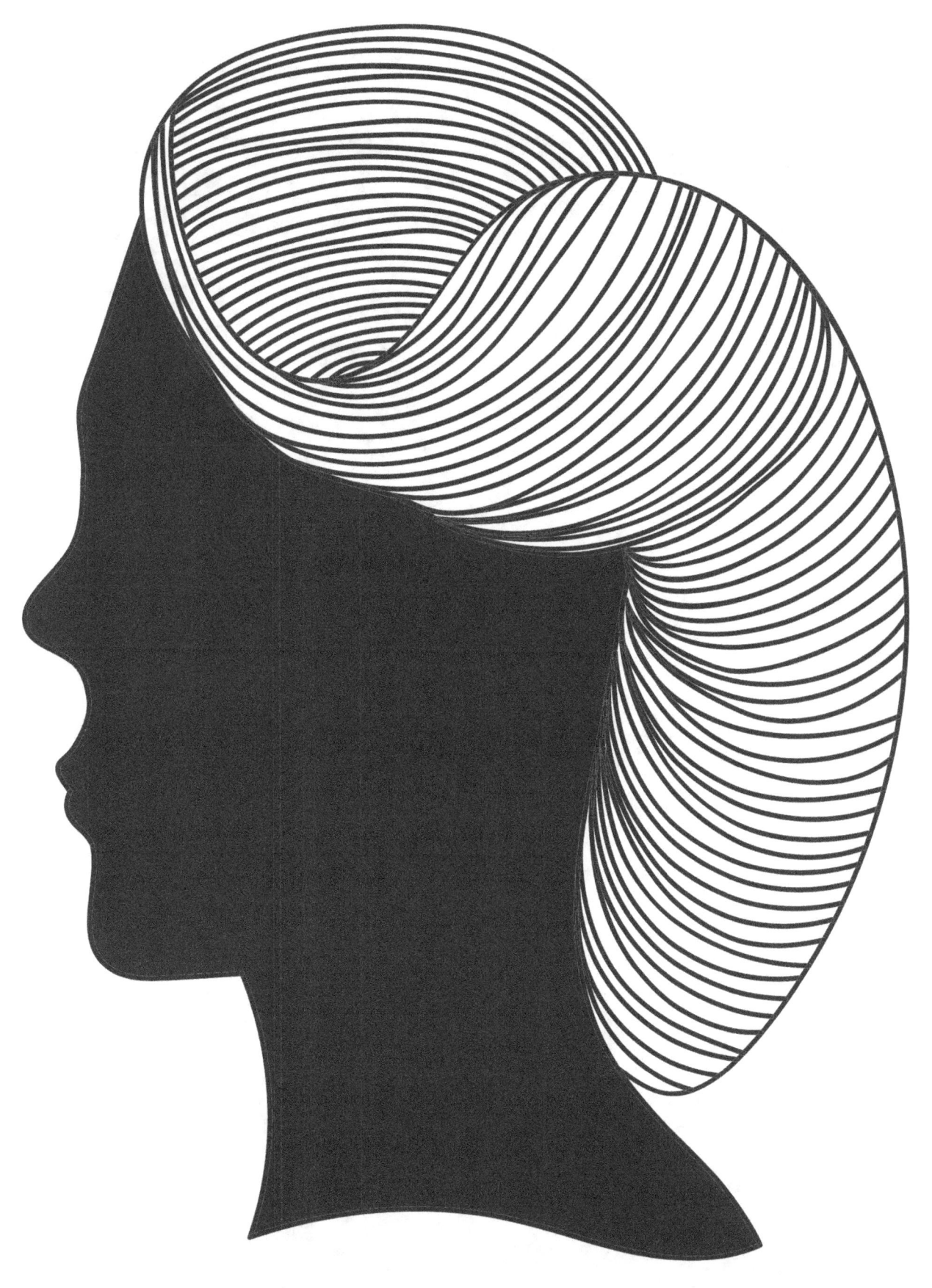

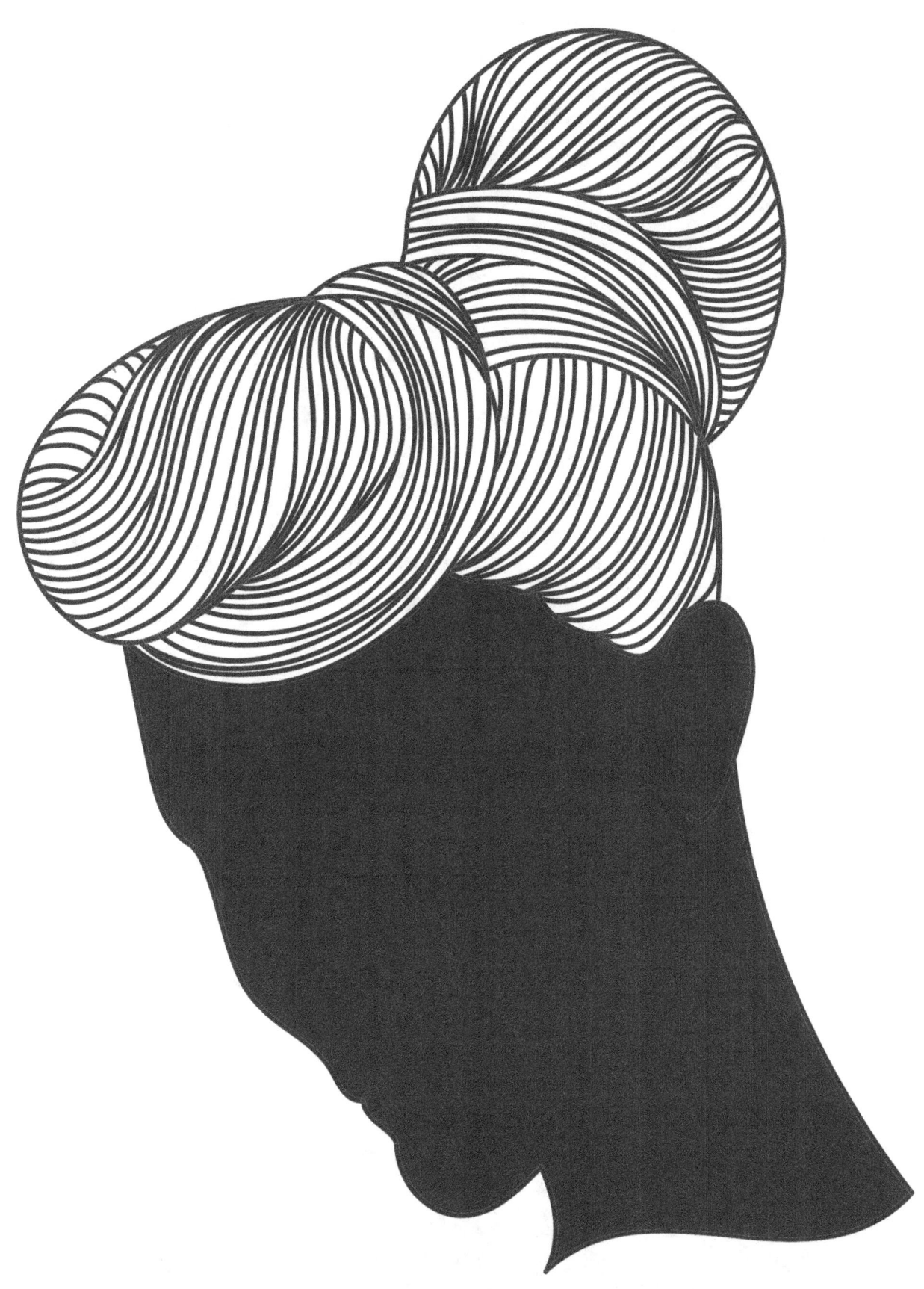

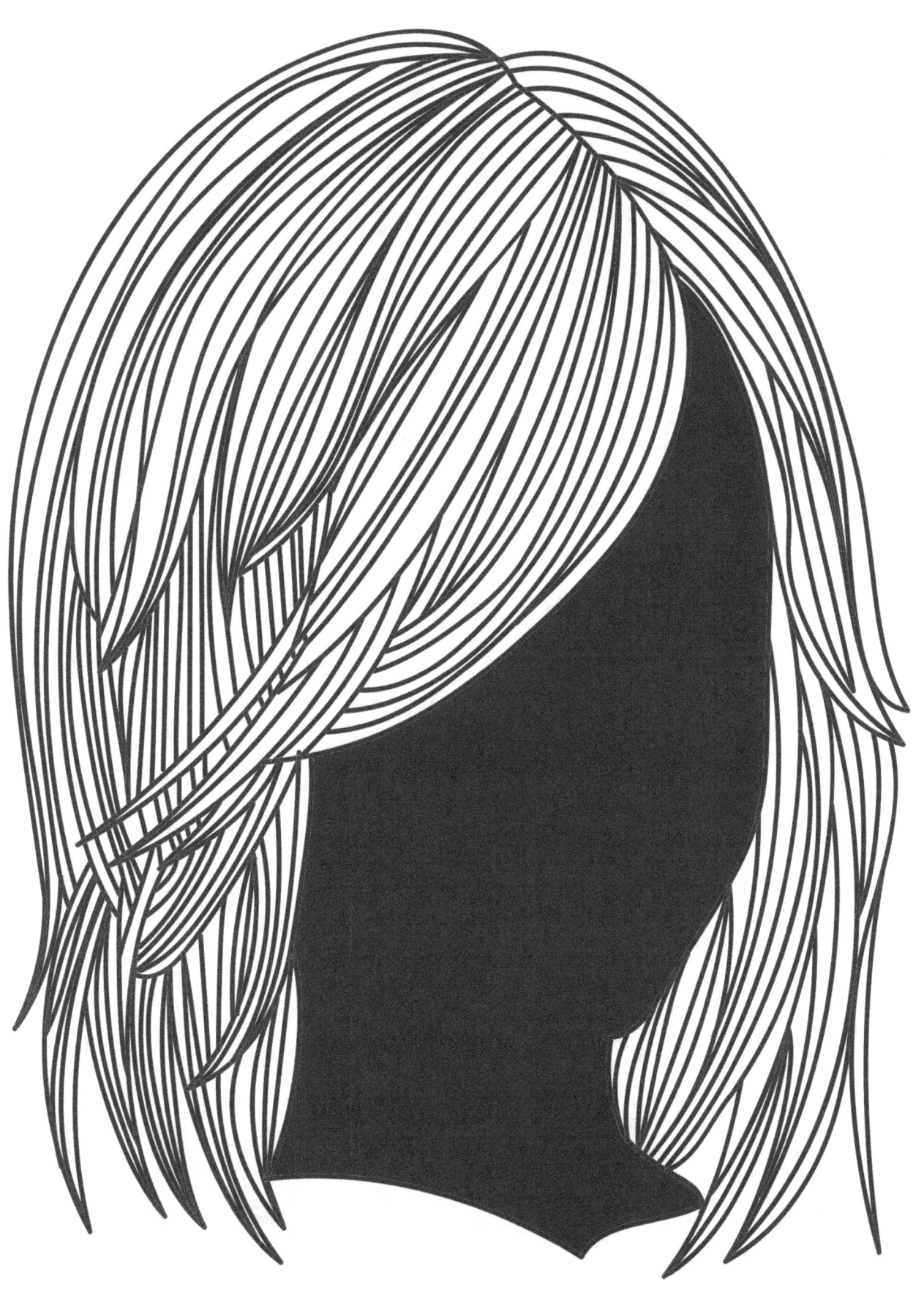

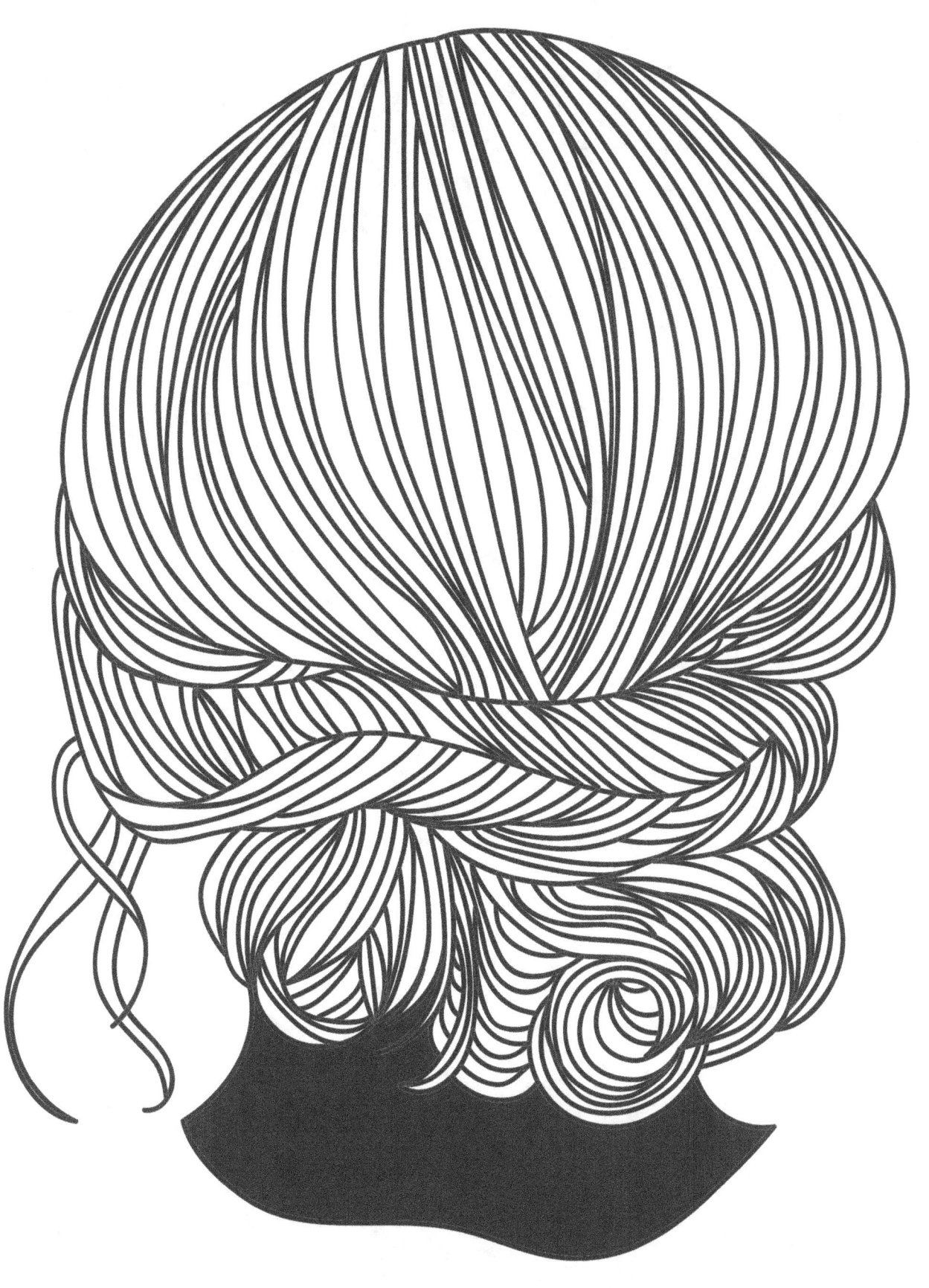

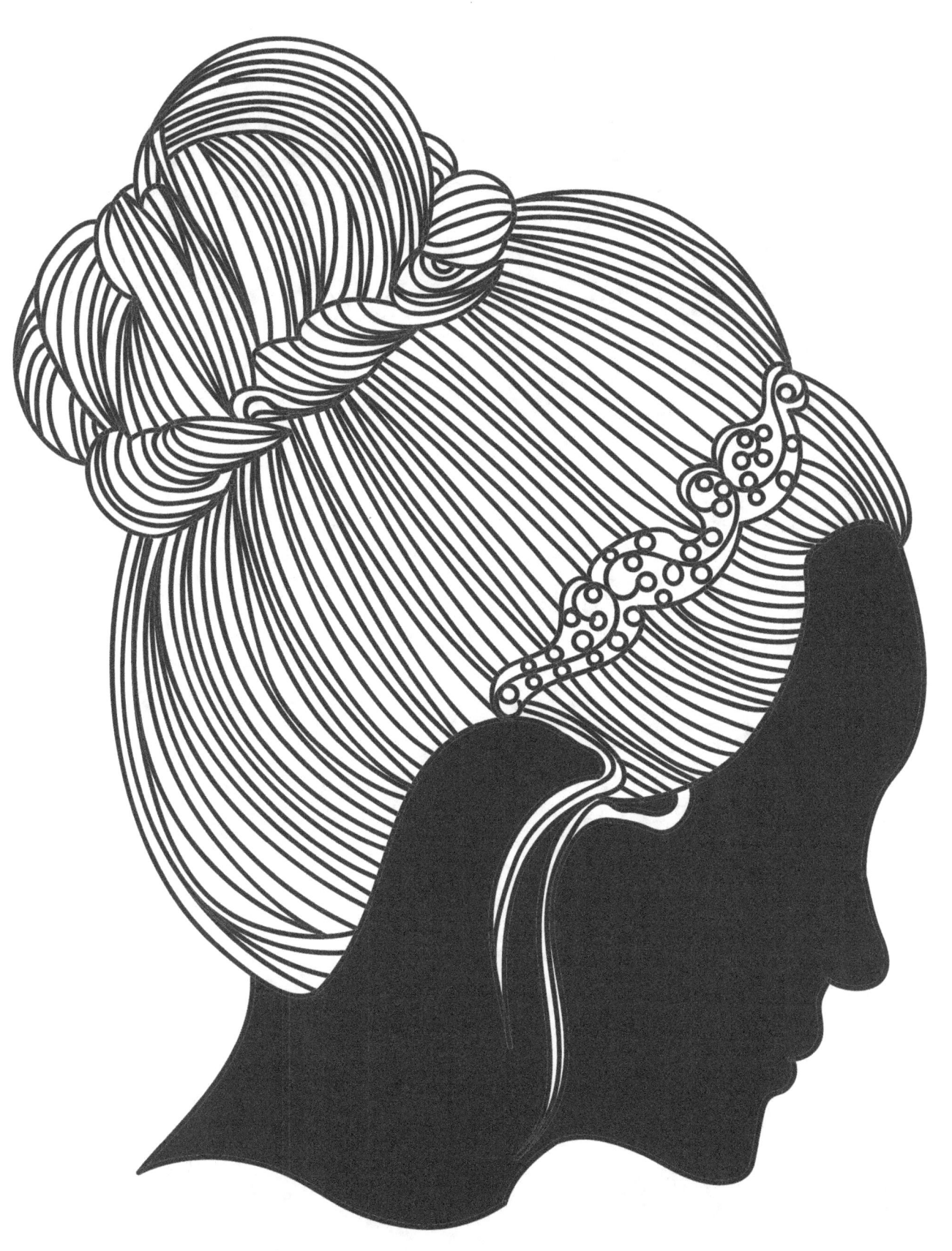

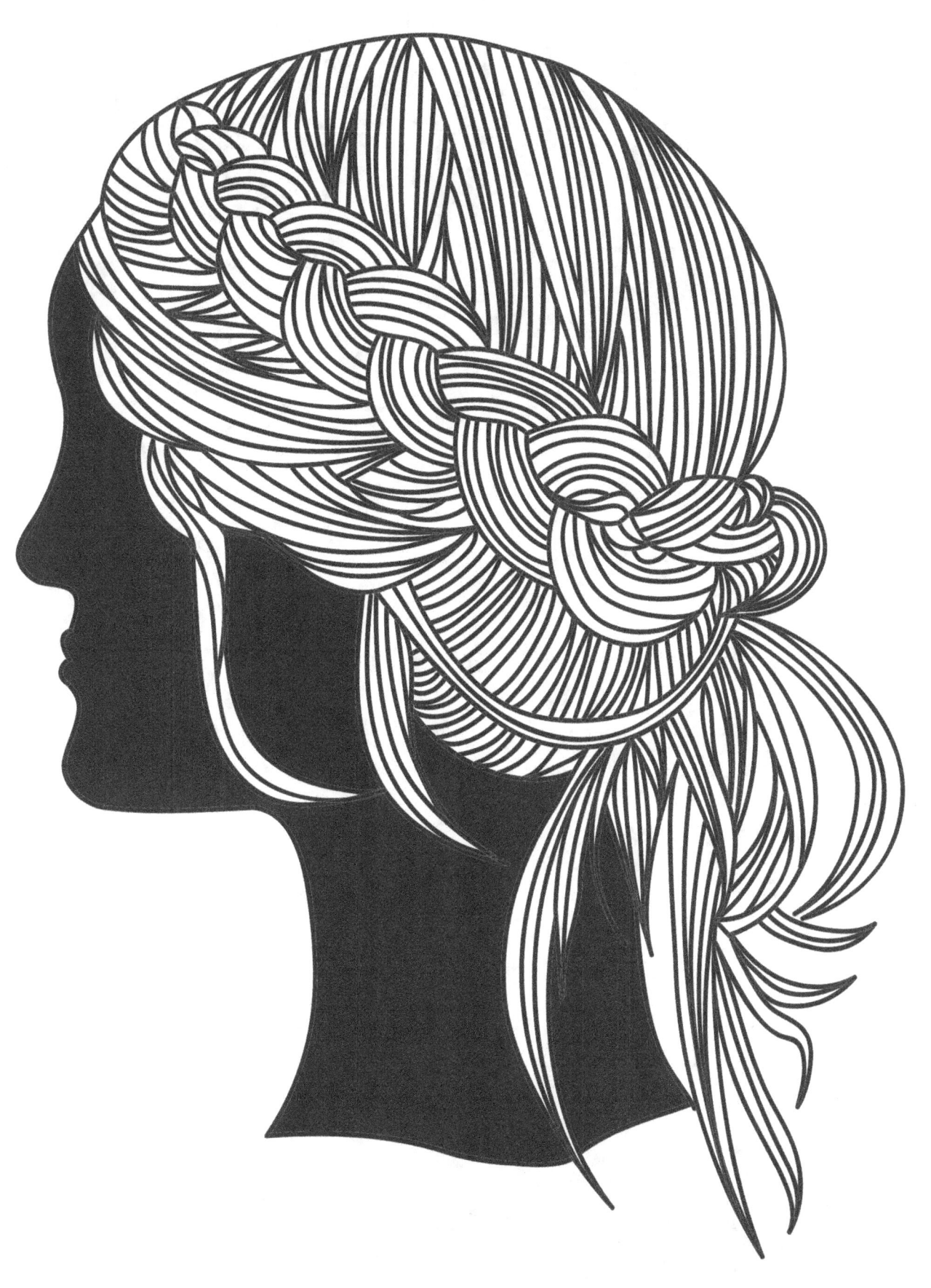

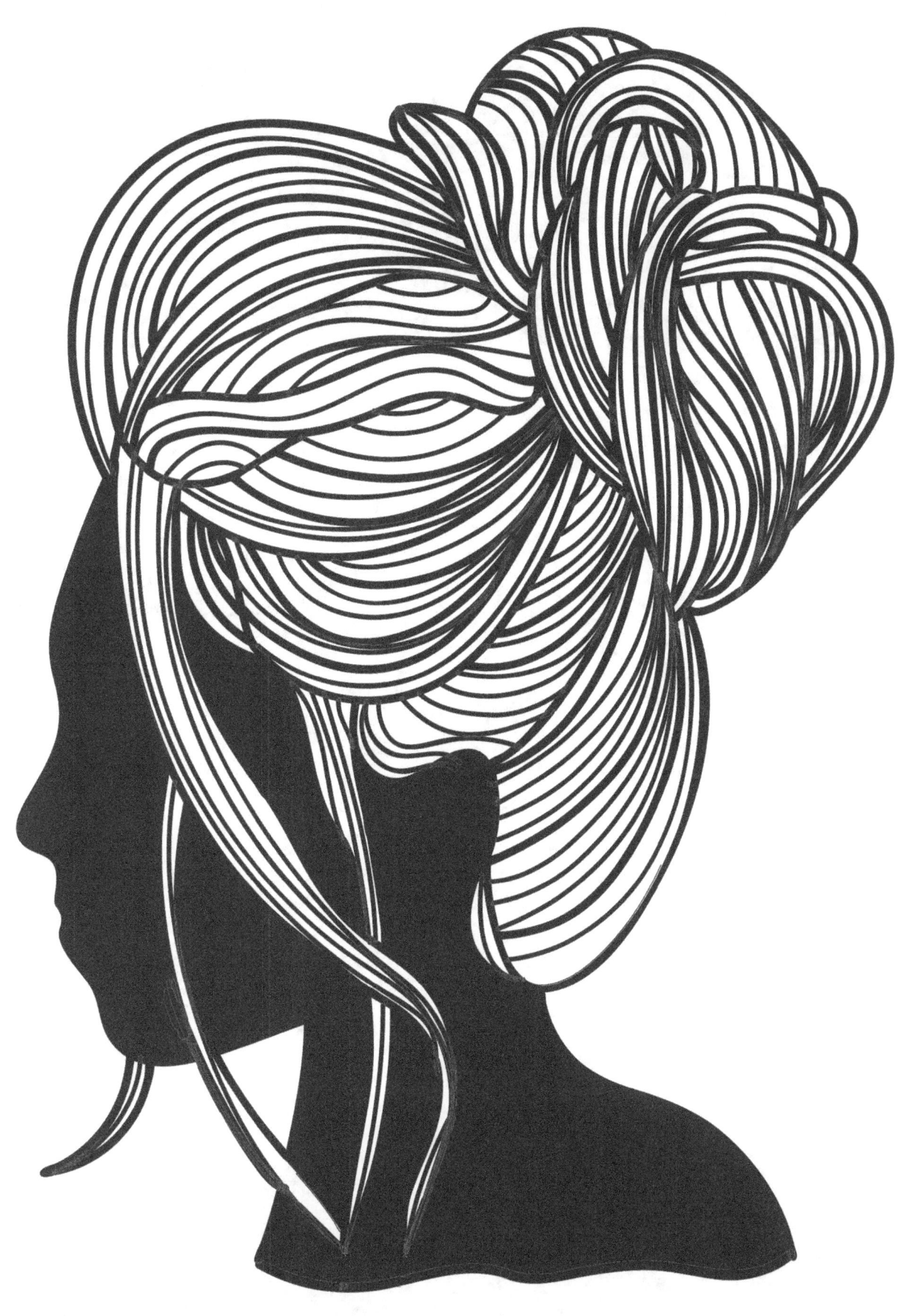

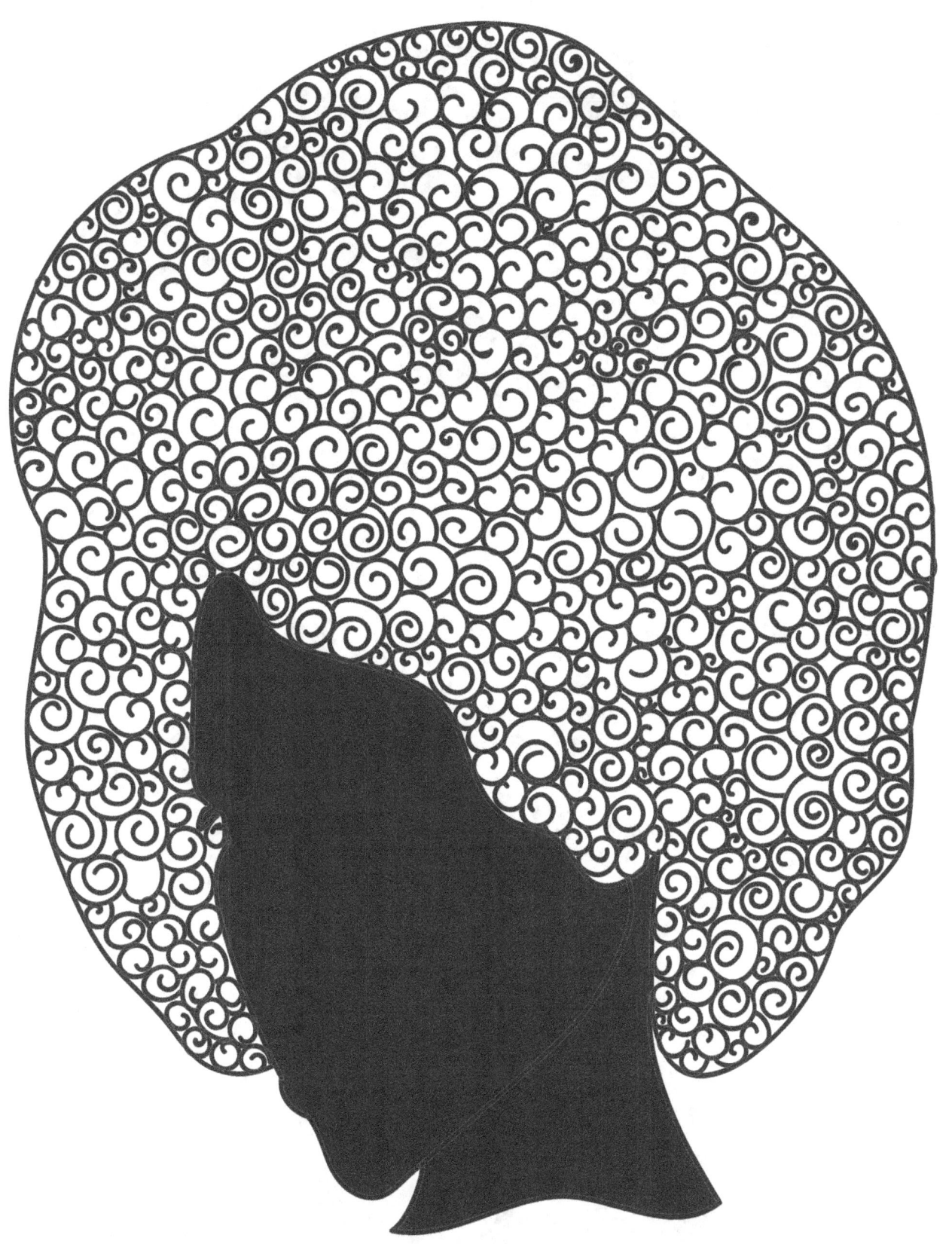

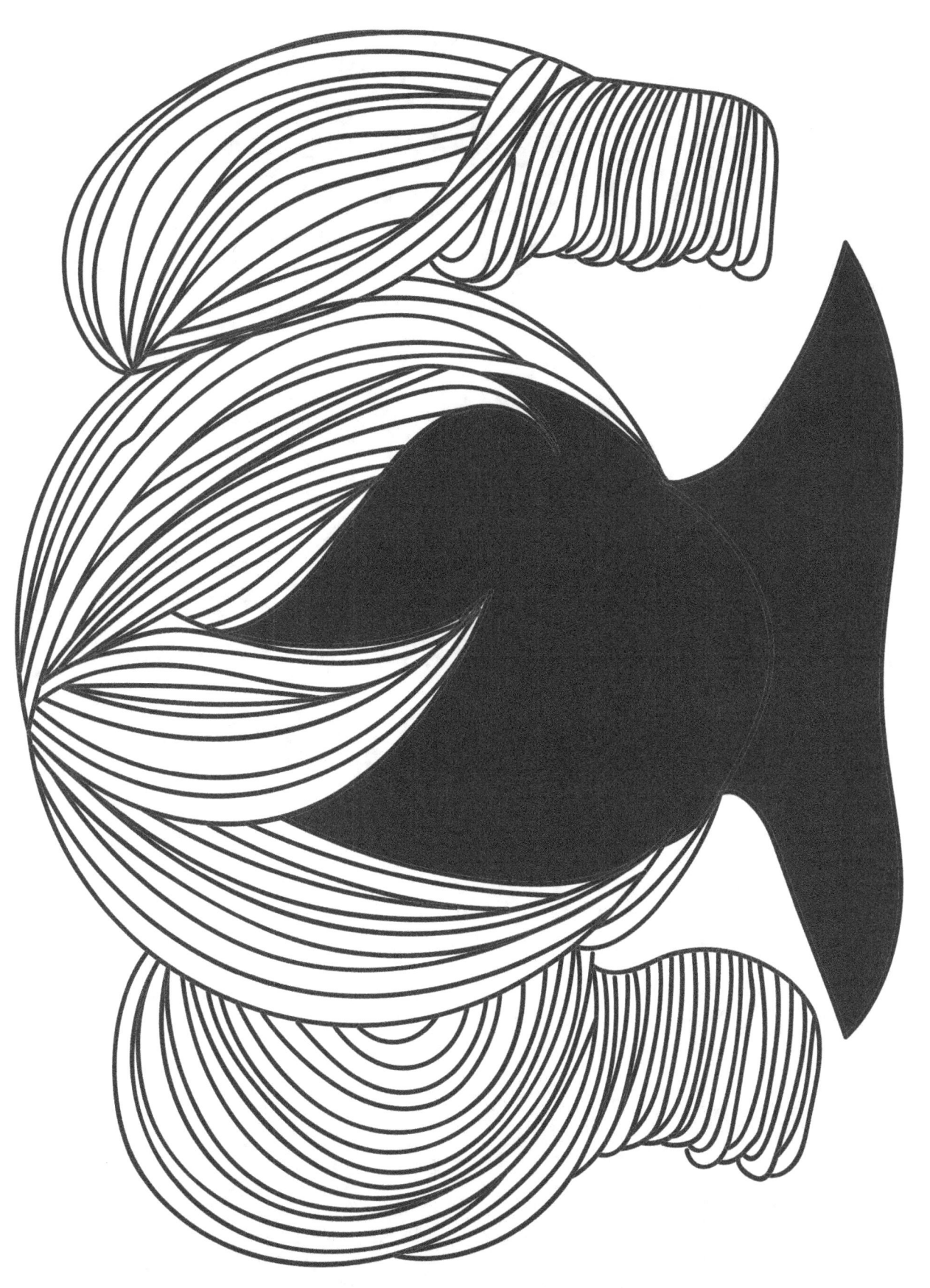

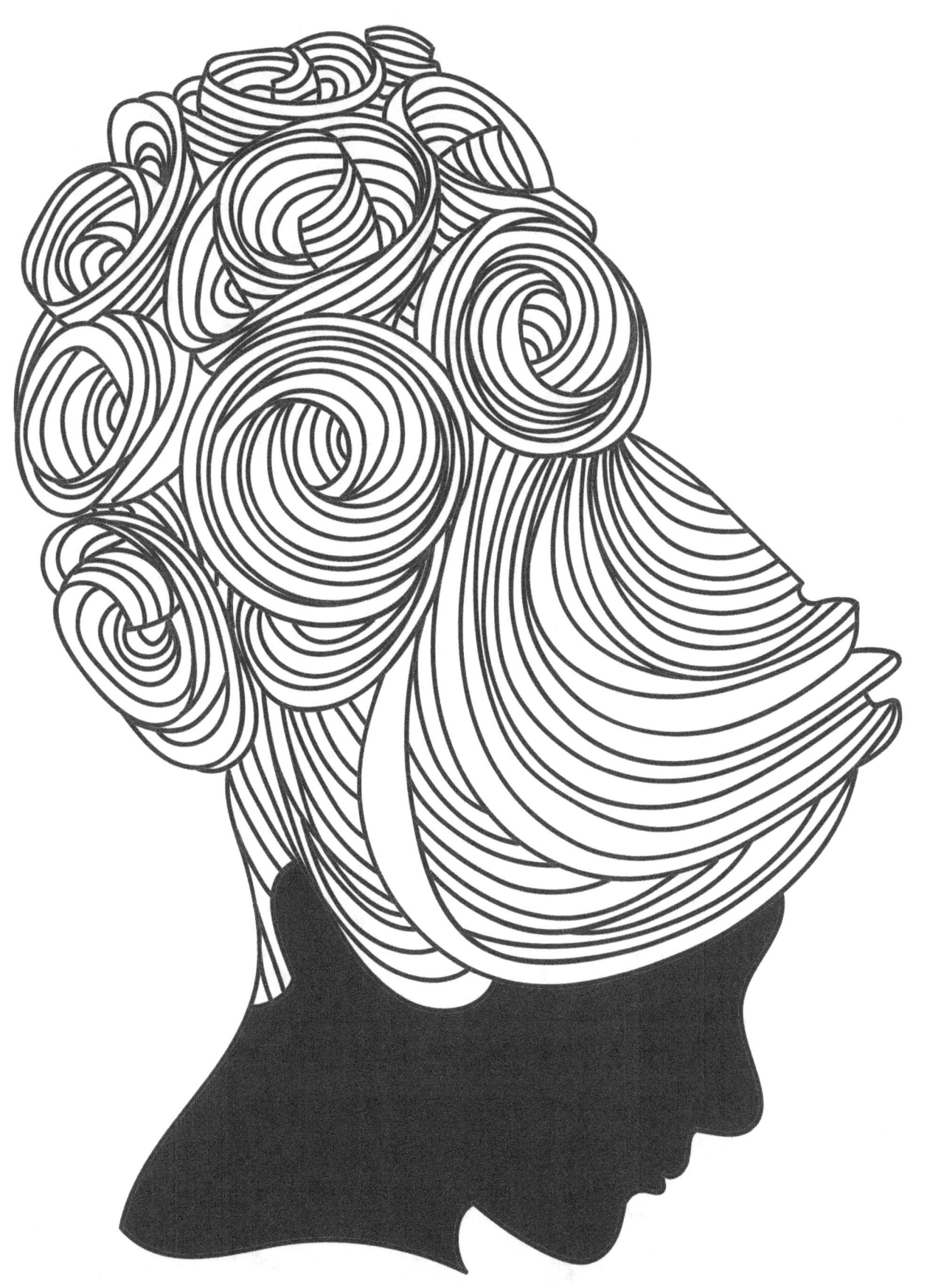

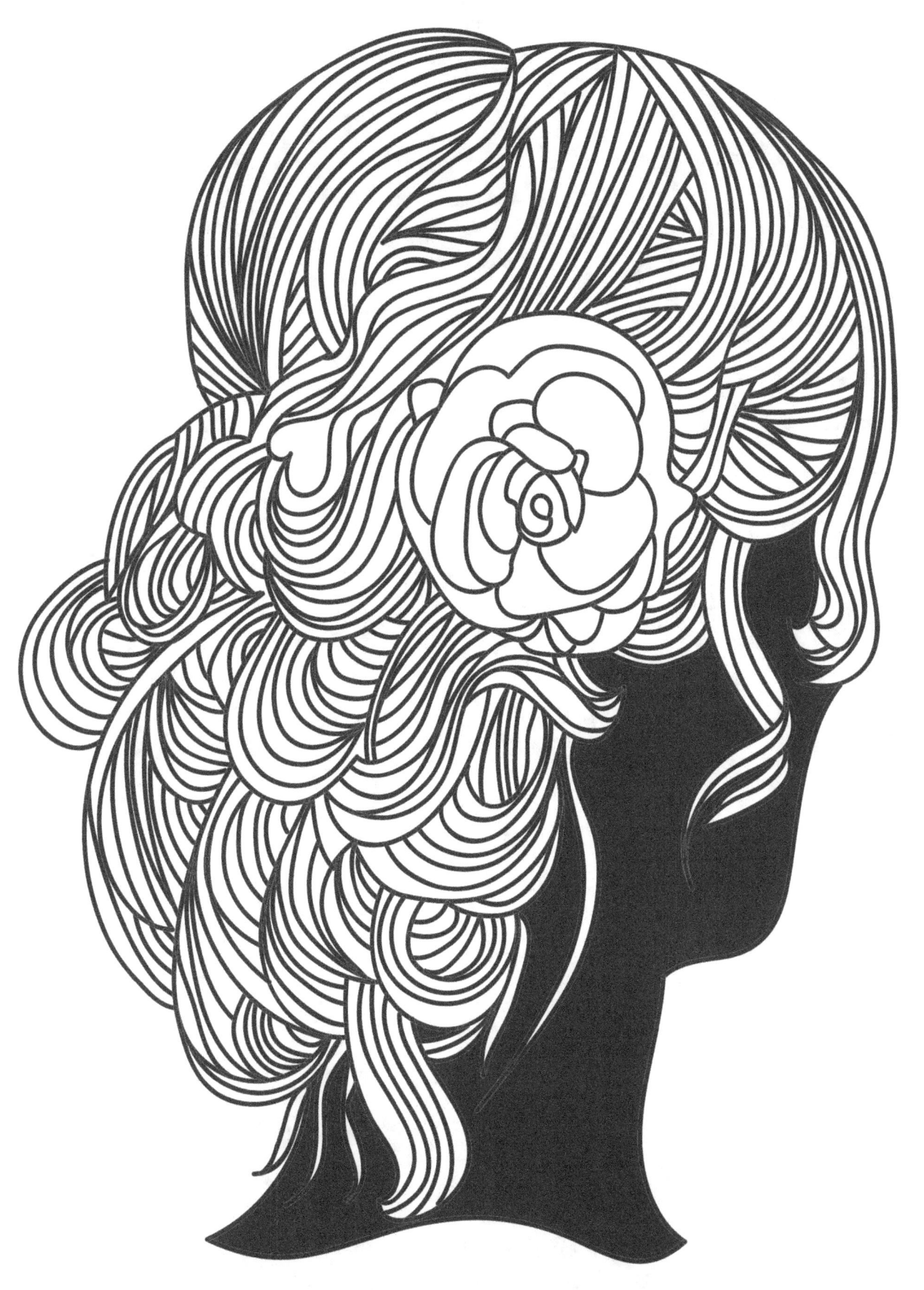

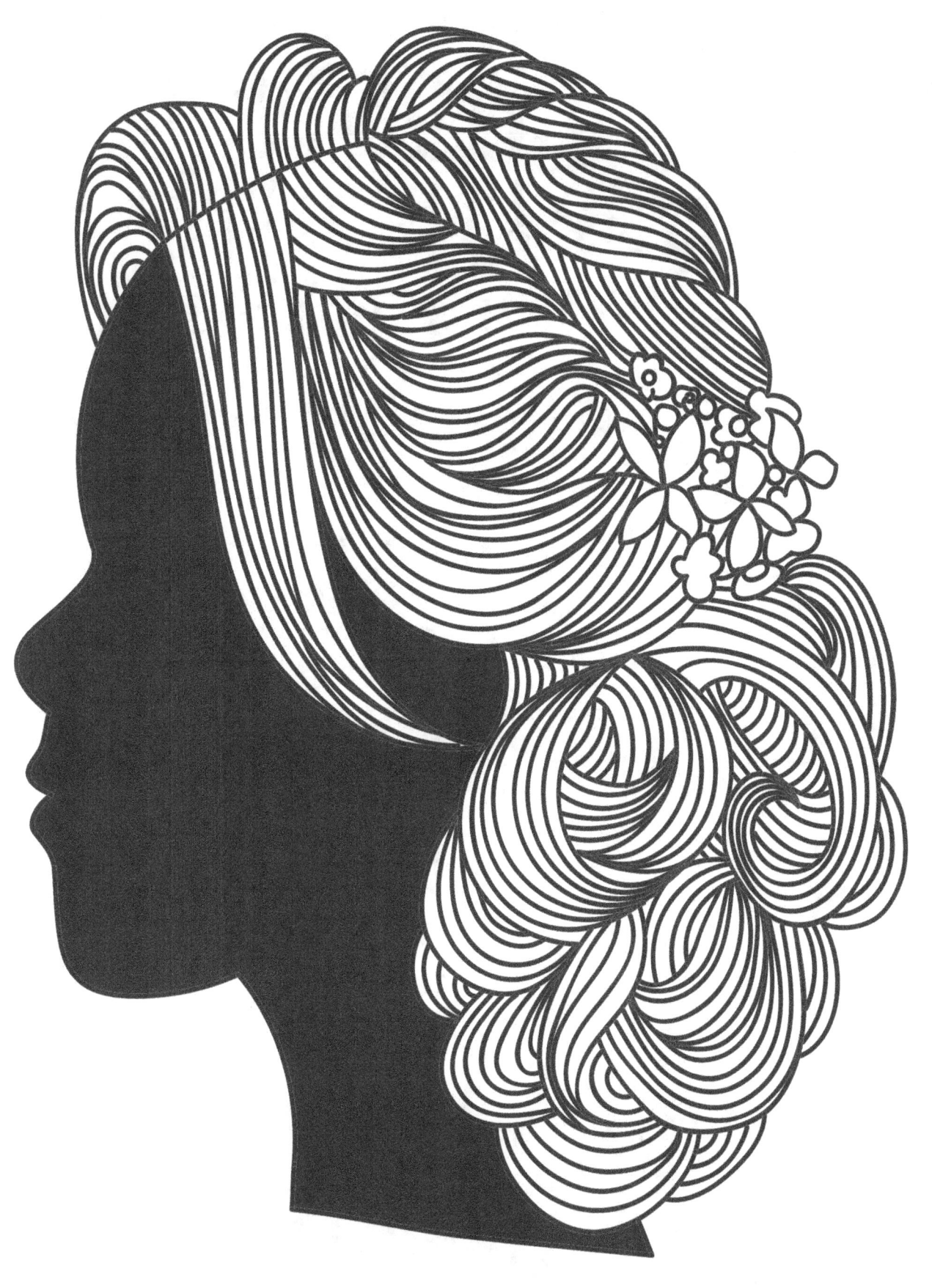

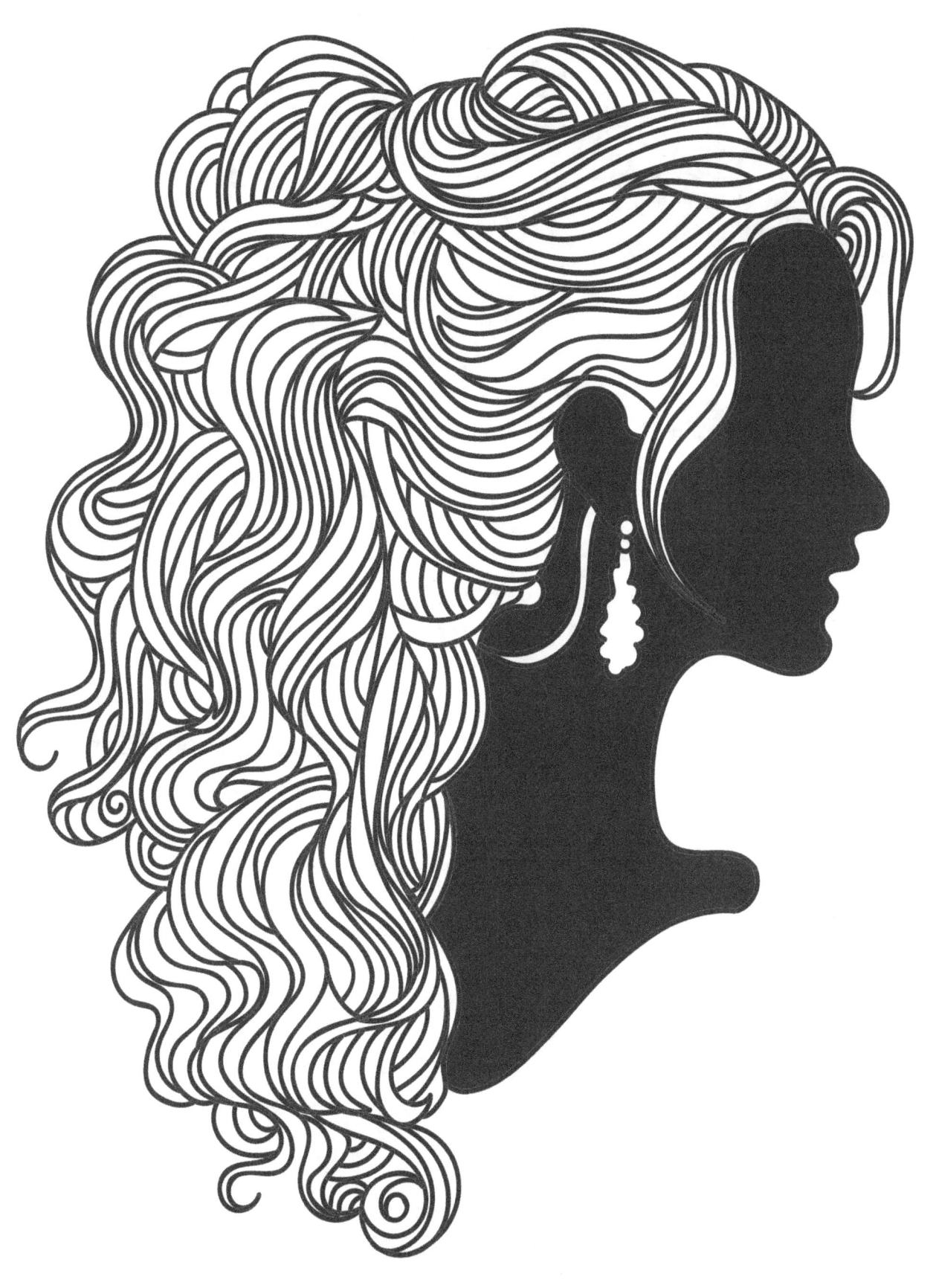

COLOR TEST PAGE

COLOR TEST PAGE

www.ingramcontent.com/pod-product-compliance
Lightning Source LLC
Chambersburg PA
CBHW081253180526
45170CB00007B/2411